seed

boosting employment through
small enterprise development

Women Entrepreneurs
in Pakistan

How to improve their bargaining power

by
Nabeel A. Goheer

InFocus Programme on Boosting Employment
through **S**mall **E**nterpris**E** **D**evelopment
International Labour Office, Geneva
and

ILO, Islamabad

ILO South Asia Advisory Team (SAAT), New Delhi

ILO
Women entrepreneurs in Pakistan: How to improve their bargaining power
Geneva, International Labour Office, 2003

ISBN 92-2-113628-0

Printed in Pakistan

Foreword

The International Labour Organization's Area Office in Islamabad and the South Asia Advisory Team (ILO-SAAT) based in New Delhi, in association with its InFocus Programme on Boosting Employment through Small Enterprise Development (IFP/SEED), are pleased to publish this report on *"Women Entrepreneurs in Pakistan: How to improve their bargaining power"*. This report presents information on an area that has hitherto not received much attention in Pakistan. The report highlights the constraints facing women entrepreneurs in business, reviews their operating environment, describes the predominant gender inequalities, and most interestingly provides the narrative stories of some 20 women selected from various economic backgrounds and family situations.

With reference to the economic recession in Pakistan, there is a pressing need to empower women economically and to create employment opportunities and income generating activities to enable them to survive, prosper and provide support for their families. For the development of women-to-women business potential, women entrepreneurs require support in the form of training in strategic business development, access to credit funds, and assistance with marketing skills, product design and development.

The report's recommendations can now be taken in association with those suggested by the key stakeholders and women entrepreneurs who participated on the ILO's workshop in Lahore on February 15, 2002. Together, these recommendations are useful in mapping out ways and means for targeting and strengthening the capacity building of women entrepreneurs, formulating training and support packages, and providing training to women councillors at district and tehsil level. The Small and Medium Enterprises Development Agency (SMEDA) and the First Women's Bank Limited (FWBL) are also to be congratulated on the landmark achievement of opening SMEDA's *First Women's Desk* in association with First Women's Bank Limited, on the occasion of the celebration of the International Women's Day on March 8, 2002.

Mr. Nabeel Goheer and his team are to be congratulated for their persistent efforts in producing this valuable and interesting report which presents the results of the survey of 150 women entrepreneurs, and provides a situational analysis for business environment for women entrepreneurs in the three major cities of Islamabad, Rawalpindi and Lahore. This report would not have been possible without the valuable inputs and support from *Mr. Gerry Finnegan*, Senior Specialist in Women's Entrepreneurship Development in IFP/SEED, ILO Geneva, and *Ms. Jyoti Tuladhar*, the Senior Gender Specialist of ILO/SAAT, based in New Delhi. The suggestions of ILO technical colleagues will provide further important guidance for the development of future action plans to support women entrepreneurs in Pakistan. The ILO Office in Islamabad has also played an important role in conceptualizing the study and supporting the implementation of the fieldwork leading to the final report. Particular mention is made of the support provided by Ms. Samina Hasan (Programme Office) and Ms. Ameena Khan (Assistant Programme Officer).

We are grateful for the financial assistance provided for this work under the Government of the Netherlands Partnership Programme with the ILO. This topic continues to be one of the most important priority areas of work for the ILO in Pakistan, and it is hoped that the ILO can continue to work actively in the area of supporting the economic empowerment of women in Pakistan.

Mr. Johannes Lokollo	Ms. Christine Evans-Klock
Director	Director
ILO Office for Pakistan &	Infocus Programme on Boosting Employment
Liaison Office for Afghanistan	through Small Enterprise Development
Islamabad	ILO Geneva

Acknowledgements

I wish to thank ILO officials, the project team and my colleagues in the development sector who have contributed to this report in one way or another. Mr. Johannes Lokollo, Director, ILO, Islamabad and Ms. Samina Hasan, Programme Officer, ILO Islamabad were the first people with whom the idea of conducting this study was incubated. When I first met Ms. Hasan for this project I found her very eager to support this research as she believed that it would go a long way in improving an understanding of women entrepreneurs, and helping them effectively in the near future. The modalities of the research and cooperation were soon finalized as Mr. Lokollo was eager and Ms. Hasan was committed to facilitate it. Latterly, Ms. Ameena Khan was also involved in providing support to facilitate completion of the report.

The concept paper provided by the ILO was very comprehensive and captured almost all the important aspects of women entrepreneurs that were to be explored. I am grateful to Mr. Gerry Finnegan, Senior Specialist, Women's Entrepreneurship Development and Gender Equality (WEDGE), in IFP/SEED, ILO Geneva, and Ms. Jyoti Tuladhar, Senior Gender Specialist in South Asia Advisory Team (SAAT), ILO New Delhi, for their dedicated supervision of this project. I must acknowledge that both of them remained intellectually involved in the project at every stage despite their hectic schedules and other official commitments.

I am very grateful to all of the women entrepreneurs who agreed to participate in this survey. They cooperated fully in our research and I thank them for their time and for their patience. In particular I wish to acknowledge the permission granted by the twenty women entrepreneurs who are featured in the short case studies presented in Part III of this report.

I am indebted to my project team and Gallup BRB who worked very hard to carry out the field research that was the most difficult part of the project. I must not forget to thank Ms. Abida Aziz, faculty member, Aga Khan University, Karachi; Ms. Saadya Hamdani, Advisor, Royal Norwegian Embassy, Islamabad; Ms. Musarrat Bashir, Deputy Programme Manager, IUCN, Islamabad; Mr. Sohail Ahmed, Programme Officer, JICA, Pakistan; and Mr. Arshed Bhatti, Section Officer, Planning Commission of Pakistan, Islamabad, for their comments and inputs into the research questionnaire. And last but not least my wife, Tasneem Saad, who kept me going by providing assistance in data collection, analysis and secretarial support, in addition to her work on the household chores. I sincerely hope that the outcome of this study will be the starting point of many tangible projects for women entrepreneurs in Pakistan.

Nabeel A. Goheer
Islamabad

Preface

This report is the outcome of a research study initiated and financed by ILO. It is aimed at obtaining a better understanding of Pakistani women entrepreneurs and their problems. The report has been organized into two parts. The first section starts with a portrayal of the specific business environment for women. A probing analysis shows that it has taken shape as a result of a complex interplay of different factors that ultimately result in the disadvantaged status of women in society, which restricts their mobility, economic participation and business activity. A chronological review of development planning in Pakistan follows. It reveals that national gender planning in Pakistan has remained hostage to the welfare approach in its first phase, and devoid of any true commitment to gender in the second phase. The next section reinforces the arguments already put forward by providing statistical comparisons of the poor gender equity record of Pakistan at national, regional and international levels. The comparisons portray a dismal picture of Pakistan and validate the analysis made in the first section. What follows is an overview of policy and institutional initiatives of the Government of Pakistan for the economic empowerment and business development of women. This appraisal has also been carried out at two levels. The first level describes developmental interventions for the relatively lower strata of micro-businesses, while the second details developmental institutions that target small and medium-sized business and emphasizes their weak gender focus. The first part ends with a complete picture of the supply side, including the business environment, a chronology of development planning, national and international benchmarking, and a description of institutional initiatives.

The second part of the report is subdivided into two sections. The first section describes the research framework and associated issues. The second section which is the major body of the report gives a detailed description of primary data gathered through a fieldwork survey of 150 women entrepreneurs. The survey explores many structural aspects of women's business in Pakistan. It also tries to capture gaps in the supply-side services, ascertains their business-related demand, and provides first-hand knowledge about the perceptions of women entrepreneurs on multiple issues. It ends with a set of recommendations that are based on the results of the survey.

The third and last part of this report is comprised of narrative stories of 20 selected women entrepreneurs from varied economic backgrounds, diverse family set-ups, and different professions. Each story is unique in itself as it reveals diverse issues related to a particular history of the start and scaling up of that business.

Nabeel A. Goheer
Islamabad

Table of contents

Abstract

This report is based on a survey of 150 women entrepreneurs in Pakistan, and covered the three major cities of Islamabad, Lahore and Rawalpindi. The sample was comprised of women entrepreneurs from a variety of sectors. In constructing the sample, the women entrepreneurs had to meet specific criteria: the women had to already be in business, they had to be operating from dedicated business premises outside of the home, and they had to be employing a minimum of 5 persons. In the study, efforts were made to determine the attitudes and commitment of the women to growing and expanding their enterprises. The report also describes the barriers and constraints, as well as the support and opportunities facing these women entrepreneurs. In addition to the quantitative findings, the report provides a brief pen picture of 20 of the women entrepreneurs. It provides updates based on an ILO conference held in February 2002 at which the preliminary findings were discussed and a set of recommendations formulated. Based on this information, a summary project proposal has been prepared by the ILO, and this is also included in the report.

PART I

1. Situational analysis of women entrepreneurs in Pakistan: Supply-side issues

1.1 The business environment for women entrepreneurs

1.1.1 *Conceptual framework*

Women entrepreneurs do not operate in isolation. They work under the same macro, regulatory and institutional framework as their male counterparts in a free market mechanism in Pakistan. It is necessary to dig deeper to understand the gender biases embedded in society which limit women's mobility, interactions, active economic participation and access to business development services.

The business environment for women in Pakistan reflects the complex interplay of many factors, which fall into two basic categories. The first is made up of social, cultural, traditional and religious elements. This aspect of the environment has taken shape over many centuries: it is anchored in the patriarchal system and clearly manifested in the lower status of women. The gender bias of this type of system is rigid and deep-rooted as it draws legitimacy from the perpetuation of a traditional mind-set, established rituals and a firm belief system.

The second group of factors derives from the first group, taking the form of constitutional structures, policy documents, regulatory arrangements and institutional mechanisms. This category is contemporary rather than traditional, so it is cosmetically impartial. The traditional systems pose difficulties for women in general and entrepreneurs in particular in two ways. First, they are inherently discriminatory; and second, they inhibit the equity-based composition of modern institutions and their fair working, as modern institutions are derived from traditional ones.

The social and cultural picture — with slight variations according to geographical region and social class — perpetuates a traditional patriarchal structure with compartmentalized gender roles. The stereotyped functions of reproduction and production assigned to women and men determine the overall ambiance of Pakistani society and also establish the status of both sexes. The reproductive role limits women to the home, where they bear children and raise the family, playing only an auxiliary part in production activity. The tradition of male honour associated with the chastity of their female relations restricts women's mobility, limits social interaction and imposes a check on their economic activity. The social, cultural and traditional taboos on women allow men to carve legitimacy for themselves in public affairs, as well as in the sphere of production and related economic activity.

The modern institutional environment has a cosmetic tinge of equality and sometimes even discriminates positively in favour of women, but the underlying power of tradition and the vested interests of the patriarchal system work to maintain the status quo. The legal framework, the policy environment and the regulatory structures thus embed — or are interpreted — to discriminate against the economic activity of women. Article 25 of the Constitution of Pakistan (1973), for example, guarantees equality of rights to all citizens irrespective of sex, race and class and also empowers the government to take action to protect and promote women's rights. But contemporary legislation covertly discriminates against women's economic activity as producers and providers of services.[1] The policy and regulatory environments are cosmetically better as they sometimes positively discriminate in favour of women. The most recent example is the draft

---

[1] Several discriminatory laws have a negative impact on women. The Hudood Ordinance of 1979, for example, equates rape with adultery and hence restricts the mobility of women. The unequal laws of inheritance (females entitled to half the share of male offspring) puts them at a disadvantage regarding initial capital to start an economic activity.

Labour Policy of the Government of Pakistan that pays lip service to female labour force issues without announcing any tangible steps to redress the problems of women workers.[2]

The regulatory environment does not generally discriminate against women, but even well-intentioned provisions can sometimes result in negative discrimination. An example would be the highly skewed labour structure of the apparel industry in Pakistan. Employment figures show that about 90 per cent of workers in this sector are male.[3] This is exactly opposite to the situation in other South Asian countries where 90 per cent of workers in the apparel industry are women. The difference is explained by a labour regulation in Pakistan that restricts the employment of women after 7 p.m. Hence the long hours often required in this industry provide a disincentive to employ women. The problem is further compounded by the complex interplay of traditional and contemporary factors. The male head of a Pakistani family would not allow his female relations to work in a factory after sunset. The domestic responsibilities of women workers make it impossible for them to work long hours outside the home. Employers do not like to hire women who might ask for maternity leave/benefits. And last but not least, women trainees would not be welcome at all the production places where Ustad-Shagird is the predominant mode of apprenticeship.[4]

1.1.2 Perceptions of women in Pakistan

The common perceptions of Pakistani women in general and their economic participation in particular reflect what has been said in the previous paragraphs. The World Bank *Country Gender Profile of Pakistan* deplores the fact that the status of women in Pakistan is among the lowest in the world.[5] UNDP (1996) describes the strong "inside/outside" dichotomy in Pakistan, where women are restricted to the "inside" space of home and household, embodied in the tradition of veiling. This restricts women's access to education, employment, training opportunities and social services.[6] Samina (1997) highlights another important aspect by stating that the social disapproval of women working outside the home translates into the invisibility of women in the labour force. Although they participate actively in the family and farm affairs, their unpaid work is perceived as a social duty rather than an economic contribution.[7] Stiglitz (1998) in his paper on gender has lamented the poor indicators of Pakistan compared with other developing countries.[8]

1.1.3 Women in development planning

Development planning in Pakistan has generally remained hostage to the welfare approach which makes women the passive recipients of the various programmes.[9] The gender aspect of development planning can be divided into different phases. The first phase started with the First Five-Year Plan (1955-60) and continued with a short break (the transition phase) until the Sixth Five-Year Plan (1983-88). In the first phase development planning treated women as the passive recipients of interventions such as skill training and income generation. No significant

---

[2] *Draft Labour Policy of the Government of Pakistan 2000*, Ministry of Labour, Manpower and Overseas Pakistanis, Government of Pakistan , Islamabad

[3] *Globalization and the apparel industry of Pakistan* presented by SMEDA at the ILO sub-regional conference on Competitiveness, Productivity and Job Quality in the Garments Industry in South Asia, 25-26 September 2001.

[4] Many studies show that the Ustad (Guru)-Shagird (disciple) relationship is the dominant mode of apprenticeship at production places in Pakistan. Most Ustads are men and they do not like to have female Shagirds: at the same time, female Shagirds prefer not to be trained by male Ustads.

[5] *Country gender profile of Pakistan*, World Bank, 1999 Washington DC.

[6] Preparatory Assistance (PA) Document Number: PAK/96/016 — *Facilitating women's mobility*, UNDP Pakistan.

[7] Samina Kamal, 1997, *Women, empowerment and poverty alleviation in South Asia: The dual benefits of Microcredit* p. 114, South Asia Poverty Alleviation Program, UNDP.

[8] Stiglitz Joseph, 1998, *Gender and development: The role of the state*, Gender and Development Workshop, Washington, DC.

[9] The Planning Commission of Pakistan in Islamabad is the hub of development planning. It draws up perspective plans for 10 years (considered as long-term planning), medium-term plans (for 5 years) and Annual Development Plans (for the fiscal year).

progress was made through small initiatives as the government programmes focused on teaching traditional skills such as sewing, embroidery, or knitting. Such training was primarily aimed at enhancing women's domestic role and had little relation to market demand and employment prospects.[10]

The transition phase started in 1973 with the advent of a secular and socialist democratic regime.[11] Medium-term planning (5-year plans) remained absent from the national scene during these years and only annual development plans were formulated and implemented. The transition phase differed from the first phase in that it was less conservative and a more liberal attitude was maintained towards women. Employment quotas were fixed for women and seats were reserved for them in the national and provincial assemblies.

The transition phase ended abruptly with the imposition of martial law in 1977 and the restoration of a conservative and fundamentalist regime. The period from 1977 to 1983 was one of the worst in the history of Pakistan when discriminatory legislation and gender bias in planning and development reached a peak.

There was another major policy shift in the Sixth Five-Year Plan (1983-88), which had a positive bias to women. That was mainly due to external pressure from international donors and partly to the social backlash that occurred due to the stringent policies of a conservative military regime. For the first time a special chapter on women in development was included in the five-year plan. This chapter reflected the findings of a working group of 28 professional women and emphasized the importance of an integrated approach to improving the status of women. The Seventh (1988-93) and Eighth Five-Year Plans (1993-98) also stressed the full integration of women into society. A number of measures such as the establishment of a special unit for women (later upgraded as the Ministry of Women Development) and a National Commission on the Status of Women have been taken but the lack of commitment in implementation means that there has been little change in the status of Pakistani women.

The Ten-Year Perspective Development Plan (2001-11) and the Three-Year Development Programme (2001-2004) of the Government of Pakistan emphasize micro-credit as the main approach to improving the conditions of Pakistani women.[12] A table showing the issues, strategies and programmes planned by the government is given as Appendix A to this report.

1.2   National and international comparisons

The logical outcome of a gender-biased environment is the low status and weak bargaining position of women. The sex-disaggregated comparison of national statistics and comparative regional benchmarking indicate the disadvantaged position of women who try to start or run a business in Pakistan.

Chart 1 shows trends in the Poverty of Opportunity Index (POPI) for women and men in Pakistan.[13] Graph (a) shows the acute incidence of poverty among women and demonstrates that women have always been more deprived than men. However, the downward slope for both sexes depicts an improving trend, although there is a widening gap between the two indices. The bar chart (b) was plotted by dividing POPI for females (F) by POPI for males (M) to show this

---

[10] Khan, N. S.; Shaheed, F. (1984), *Women's skill development and income generating schemes and projects in the Punjab*, Report prepared for UNICEF.

[11] The Eastern part of Pakistan became the separate country of Bangladesh in 1971. The first elected government of West Pakistan (presently Islamic Republic of Pakistan) then took office to bring radical changes in the economy and society of Pakistan.

[12] *Ten-Year Development Perspective Plan (2001-11)* and *Three-Year Development Programme (2001-4)*, Government of Pakistan, Planning Commission Islamabad, 1 September 2001.

[13] The Poverty of Opportunity Index is a composite indicator that defines poverty as a multi-faceted phenomenon. It includes other dimensions such as education and health along with the simple economic definition of poverty.

phenomenon clearly. The comparative rise in female poverty and deprivation means that women are becoming progressively poorer compared to men.

Chart 1: Disparities in opportunity

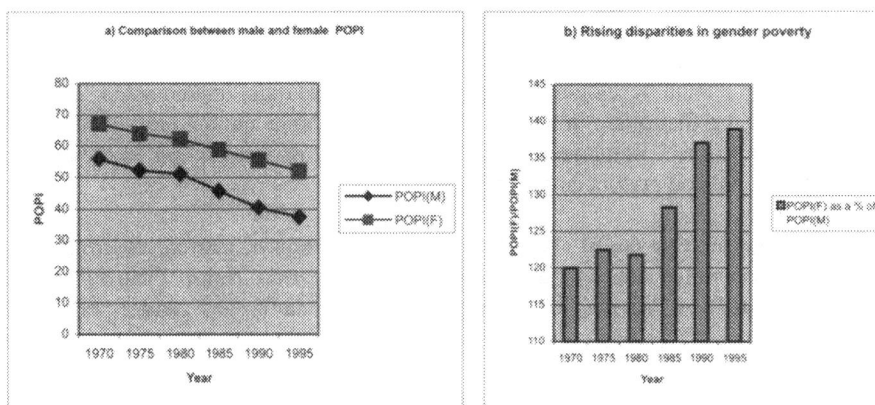

Source: Prepared from the data set of the Pakistan Poverty Monitor Project 1998

Box 1 shows some snapshots of women's participation in global labour markets, including relevant figures for Pakistan.

Box 1: Global labour market: Percentage of female labour

- In Europe, the activity rate of women in the labour market has increased in the last two decades.
- In Denmark it is 46.9 per cent.
- In the Netherlands it increased from 24.2 per cent in 1975 to 40.6 per cent in 1993.
- In the USA and Canada it grew from 37 per cent and 32 per cent respectively in 1970 to 45 per cent in 1990.
- In Pakistan it merely increased from 6.6 per cent in 1968/69 to 13.6 per cent in 1996/97.

Sources: *UNDP Human Development Report*, 1987; *World Development Report;* World Bank 200/2001; Federal Bureau of Statistics.

Chart 2 shows that the distribution of formal employment in Pakistan is heavily biased in favour of men: approximately six times more men than women work in the formal economy. The chart plots statistics obtained from the Annual Labour Force Surveys prepared by the Federal Bureau of Statistics (FBS) which surveys more than 20,000 households.[14]

---

[14] The ratio of men to women in Pakistan is around 52: 48. There is considerable debate over the low female labour force participation rate, which is well below average and much lower than in culturally similar countries like India and Bangladesh. It is broadly acknowledged though that a number of factors affect these figures. One major reason could be a non-sampling error, i.e. social sanctions against women entering the formal market inhibit housewives — additionally engaged in non-domestic activities — from declaring these activities especially to the male officials who carry out FBS surveys. In order to find out the true participation of women workers in the labour force the survey questionnaire of FBS was redrafted in the early 1990s to capture the hidden employment within households which otherwise is under-reported or invisible.

Chart 2: Gaps in employment

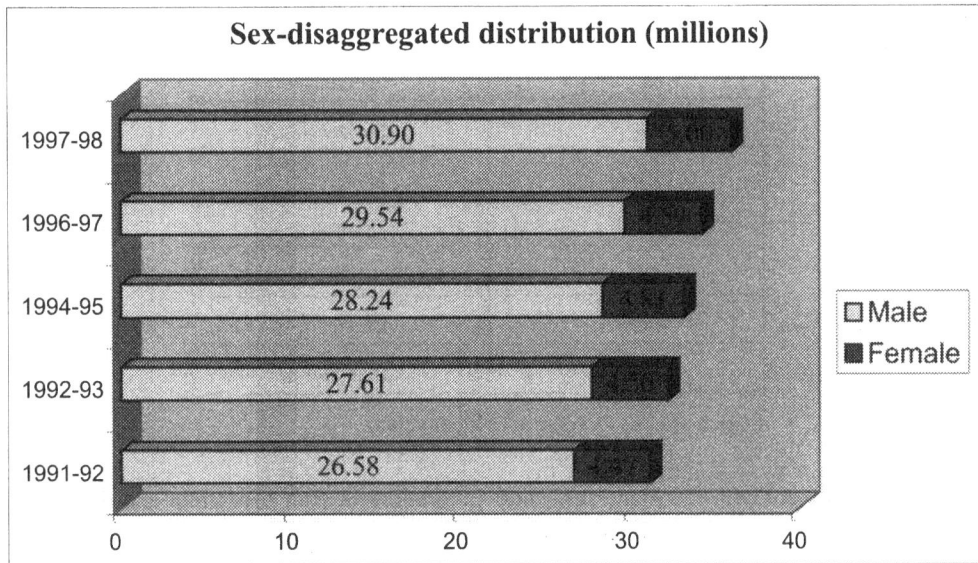

Sex-disaggregated distribution (millions)

Year	Male	Female
1997-98	30.90	
1996-97	29.54	
1994-95	28.24	
1992-93	27.61	
1991-92	26.58	

(scale: 0, 10, 20, 30, 40)

□ Male
■ Female

Source: Labour Force Surveys of Pakistan

Chart 3 shows both the crude and the improved estimates of female labour force participation, based upon earlier labour force surveys.[15] Even the improved estimates, however, show women's labour force participation to be little more than half the crude male rate.

Chart 3: Inequalities in labour force participation rates

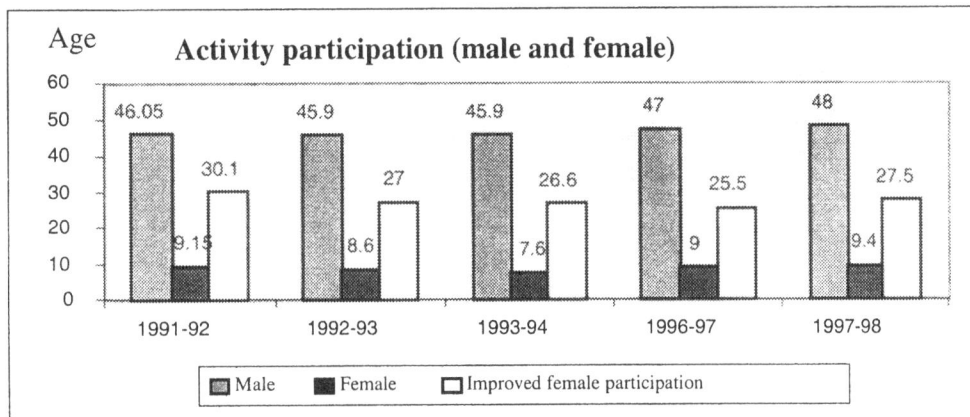

Activity participation (male and female) (Age)

	1991-92	1992-93	1993-94	1996-97	1997-98
Male	46.05	45.9	45.9	47	48
Female	9.15	8.6	7.6	9	9.4
Improved female participation	30.1	27	26.6	25.5	27.5

(scale: 0, 10, 20, 30, 40, 50, 60)

▨ Male   ■ Female   ☐ Improved female participation

Source: Labour Force Surveys of Pakistan

Pakistan ranks exactly in the middle (fourth) compared to its South Asian neighbours in the Gender Related Development Index (GDI) which is a composite index of gender disparity (shown in table 1) developed almost on the same lines as the Human Development Index.[16]

---

[15] The improved or refined participation rate corresponds to the labour force above the age of 10.

[16] HDI is a composite index of longevity, knowledge and decent standard of living.

5

Table 1: GDI rankings for South Asia

GDI rank	Country
84	Sri Lanka
89	Maldives
128	India
135	Pakistan
144	Nepal
142	Bhutan
146	Bangladesh

Source: Human Development Report 2000

In terms of GNP, Pakistan ranks third in South Asia after Sri Lanka and the Maldives. But Pakistan ranks lowest in the South Asian region in terms of GDP per capita for women. Chart 4 shows that the real GDP per capita — defined in terms of Purchasing Power Parity — for Pakistani women is the lowest in South Asia.

Chart 4: Female GDP per capita

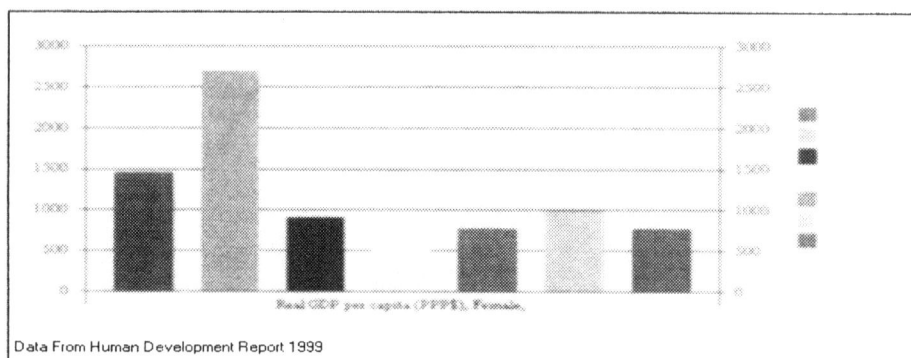

Data From Human Development Report 1999

In summary, as Dr. Akmal Hussain, a well-known economist laments:

> As a result of the inferior status of women in society, their underestimation as economic agents as well as the gender bias embedded in the development policies pursued so far, most women in Pakistan have carried a double burden, that of being poor and being women. [17]

1.3 Supply-side initiatives: An overview

The Women's Division established in 1979 as a part of the Cabinet Division was upgraded to become the Ministry of Women's Development (MoWD) in 1989. This apparently showed a government commitment to address the issues of Pakistani women in a serious way. However, the appointment of nine different secretaries between 1989 and1993 reflected a non-serious approach, a fragmented focus and inconsistent policies. [18]

---

[17] Akmal Hussain, 1994, *Poverty Alleviation in Pakistan*, Vanguard Books, Lahore, Pakistan.
[18] *Women and the Pakistan Government: A brief policy history (1975-1998)* UNDP, Islamabad.

The Government of Pakistan signed the Convention on the Elimination of all forms of Discrimination Against Women (CEDAW) in 1995. A National Plan of Action was prepared and issued in 1998 by the MoWD, which detailed the strategic objectives of 12 targeted areas and their respective plans. The Government of Pakistan (GoP) and Pakistani NGOs participated in the Beijing +5 meeting in New York and submitted two reports on the initiatives taken by the respective sectors on the 12 areas of the National Plan of Action. Appendix C to this report provides an extract from the government report that describes initiatives taken by the public sector in two areas, viz. "Women and Poverty" and "Women and the Economy". Appendix D provides the same information from the NGO sector. An update on the Government of Pakistan's programme for the development and empowerment of women (as at December 2002) has been included as Appendix B of this report.

1.3.1 Initiatives for subsistence (micro) businesses

The last decade has seen a number of initiatives using micro-credit as a tool for poverty alleviation. Examples include the Pakistan Poverty Alleviation Fund (PPAF), the National Rural Support Programme (NRSP), other Rural Support Programmes (RSPs), and more recently the Khushali Bank. These programmes have tried to target women in their lending programmes for two reasons. First, because the success of micro-credit in Bangladesh is partly linked with lending to women borrowers whose conservative and trustworthy behaviour has made it possible for the bank to sustain its lending operations.[19] Second, the rising levels of poverty in Pakistan and the preponderance of poor women have forced policy makers to give special attention to women who intend to start a tiny or micro business activity. It is ironical, though, that despite this "focus" the best ever outreach recorded for the RSPs is a 25 per cent coverage of women as borrowers. These programmes have so far disbursed Rs. 5164 million (equivalent to around US$ 85 million) as micro-credit to 852, 636 beneficiaries with an average loan of US$ 100.[20] The male to female ratio of the major programmes is as follows:[21]

- Aga Khan Rural Support Programme (AKRSP)   = 91:09
- National Rural Support Programme (NRSP)   = 80:20
- Punjab Rural Support Programme (PRSP)   = 77:23

NGO programmes offer micro-credit to women much more frequently than the RSPs but their overall coverage is very small. A recent World Bank study reveals that only three NGOs had disbursed micro-credit to more than 1000 clients by March 2001.[22] The Agricultural Development Bank of Pakistan (ADBP) which is the largest development finance institution in the country has also started a small-scale credit scheme for women. A special lending programme called the Agricultural Credit Programme (ACP) includes group guarantees like those of the Grameen Bank, acceptance of gold as a substitute for land collateral and female/male small teams of Mobile Credit Officers (MCOs). Shahnaz regrets that after more than 3 years of operation, only 4,700 women had obtained loans under this scheme.[23]

The micro-credit programmes focus on the survival skills of the beneficiaries and their major thrust is on poverty alleviation. However, the scope of the present study is different, as it is intended to address a relatively higher strata that is in commercial business. A description of lower strata (poverty alleviation initiatives) has been included as it is understood that subsistence business cannot be divorced from micro, small and medium-size business. The following part of

---

[19] This argument is with reference to the Grameen Bank of Bangladesh which has emerged as a role model for such interventions as more than 90 per cent of borrowers have traditionally been women.

[20] US $1 = Rs. 61.

[21] *Rural Support Programme Network (RSPN)*, F 6/4, Islamabad , Pakistan.

[22] Naseem, S.M., *Government and NGO Programmes in the alleviation of poverty in Pakistan*, Draft report submitted to the World Bank, Pakistan, March 2001.

[23] Shahnaz Kazi, *Gender inequalities and development in Pakistan*, in *50 years of Pakistan's economy* ed. Rafi Kahn, Shahrukh, Oxford University Press 2000, Islamabad.

the situation analysis deals exclusively with institutions which facilitate small and medium-size enterprises (SMEs).

1.3.2 SME initiatives

The paragraphs below provide a brief description of all those institutions (financial and non-financial) that have been created by the provincial and federal governments for the promotion of small and medium enterprises.

Punjab Small Industries Corporation (PSIC)

The Punjab Small Industries Corporation (PSIC) was established in 1972 as an autonomous body for the promotion and development of small and cottage industry in the Punjab province. It is larger than its counterparts in other provinces and has traditionally engaged in developing industrial estates, establishing Common Facility Centres (CFCs), lending for investment and working capital, and providing guidance for technology transfer. Most PSIC activities have not focused on women entrepreneurs. There were some attempts to start specific programmes but the results fell short of expectations. For example, an evaluation of the Women's Craft Development Centres of PSIC which was carried out by a group of consultants disclosed their poor performance in developing crafts, as well as in design, training and marketing. The promotion of entrepreneurship was mentioned as the weakest aspect of the programme.[24]

Sindh Small Industries Corporation (SSIC)

The SSIC was also established in the Punjab in 1972, with almost the same mandate as that of PSIC. It has so far established 17 industrial estates and 6 artisanal colonies. It used to offer subsidized loans under a small credit scheme that was started in 1988-89. The scheme was terminated partly because of the paucity of resources and partly because lending under IMF conditionalities needs to be at market-based interest rates. The SSIC later engaged in disbursing loans under the Prime Minister's self-employment scheme. The Corporation does not have a specific gender focus and is not running projects to promote women entrepreneurs in the province.

Sarhad Small Industries Development Board (SSIDB)

The SSIDB is a sister organization of PSIC and SSIC; it was established in 1972 as a board and not as a corporation. The functions are very similar and the mandate is to promote the development of small and cottage industry. The Board has been working to develop industrial estates, train human resources, promote traditional cottage industry and disburse credit for cottage industry. Few of its programmes or activities have targeted women entrepreneurs. The policies, programmes and projects are aimed at business, which is considered a male domain in this relatively conservative province.[25] Women and households have mostly benefited indirectly from traditional business activities such as carpet weaving and Patti making. The women development programmes, which are few and far between, have trained 2,062 women in a variety of skills.

Directorate of Industries (Balochistan)

Balochistan is the largest province of Pakistan and it has the smallest population (around 5 per cent of the total). The provincial government has no corporation or board catering to the small-scale sector and cottage industry. The Directorate of Industries under the Department of

---

[24] *Identification of women's small entrepreneurship development support project in the Province of the Punjab*, submitted to the Royal Netherlands Embassy, Islamabad Pakistan by Shirkat Gah and Entrepreneurial Development and Advisory Services (EDAS), Lahore (No date mentioned).

[25] North Western Frontier Province (NWFP) known in the local language as "Sarhad". Sarhad and Balochistan form the western frontier with Afghanistan. The majority of the population shares ethnic and cultural ties with the bordering country and is predominantly conservative.

Industries, Commerce and Minerals looks after the development of small and cottage enterprises. Owing to the size of the province it has 63 training centres that teach traditional skills. These centres have trained 2,750 persons in carpet weaving; 450 in Balochi embroidery; 500 in leather embroidery; 375 in tailoring and cutting; 350 in handloom weaving; 200 in woodwork; 225 in marble work, and 1,500 in other skills. There is hardly any history of special projects for women entrepreneurs, but a majority of trainees in carpet weaving have been women. Presently 361 women are being trained in these centers.[26]

Small and Medium Enterprise Development Authority (SMEDA)

SMEDA is a relatively new organization that was established in 1998 to provide a policy focus to SME activities in Pakistan. SMEDA was given a mandate to provide and facilitate support services to new and existing SMEs, coordinate policy and action frameworks for the SME sector, act as a lobby group for SMEs in the highest policy-making echelons of government, and serve as a key resource and information base for SMEs in Pakistan. SMEDA started with an emphasis on devising comprehensive strategies for some targeted SME sectors and implementing them with the help of government departments and regulatory authorities. There was a slight shift in focus in the second year of operation when SMEDA participated in a number of research studies regarding the future of different SME sectors in the wake of accession to WTO and trends in international markets. SMEDA is presently working to promote a policy framework, as well as a regulatory and institutional environment which will be conducive to SME development. (Much of the early policy work was carried out in association with ILO's IFP/SEED.) It also provides Business Development Services (BDS) to its clientèle. It has four regional offices, one in each province. To date SMEDA has undertaken no projects with an exclusive gender focus.

SME Bank

The Government of Pakistan has recently promulgated an ordinance to create the SME Bank by merging the Small Business Finance Corporation (SBFC) and the Regional Development Finance Corporation (RDFC). The new bank began operations in January 2002 as an independent company. Already the new bank has indicated that it will give a special focus to women entrepreneurs.

Small Business Finance Corporation (SBFC)

SBFC was established in 1972 to cater solely to the financial needs of small and medium business. The main thrust of the institution was always on self-employment schemes in which small entrepreneurs were provided subsidized credit for starting or running a business. However, the institution could not play its role effectively as successive governments used the subsidized credit to win political favours. The institution was on the verge of collapse with 70 per cent of non-performing loans when the new management took over in early 2000 and started a drastic restructuring. A few women entrepreneurs benefited from SBFC but the vast majority of clients were men. SBFC launched its first special scheme, the "Women Entrepreneur Development Programme" in September 2001. Under this programme women entrepreneurs could seek financial assistance within the range of Rs. 50,000 to Rs. 300,000 (US $800 to $4,800). Loans have already been sanctioned under this scheme, as part of the activities of the new SME Bank.

Regional Development Finance Corporation (RDFC)

RDFC was established in 1985 to promote industrialization in the less-developed areas of Pakistan. It had a head office in Islamabad and 14 regional branches. The Corporation financed a number of projects and also started an Industrial Credit for Rural Women (ICRW) scheme,

---

[26] Data collected from the Directorate of Industries, Government of Balochistan.

providing subsidized loans ranging from Rs. 25,000 to Rs. 200,000 to women entrepreneurs. RDFC has now been merged with the SBFC to form the SME bank.

Export Promotion Bureau (EPB)

The main objective of the Export Promotion Bureau is to promote Pakistani products and services in the international market. EPB sponsors the participation of Pakistani exporters in international exhibitions, arranges exhibitions in Pakistan, facilitates trade delegations and establishes display centres in Pakistan and abroad. There has been no specific gender focus in the policies and programmes of EPB until recently, partly because of the low participation of women in commercial activity and especially in the export business. EPB has recently been trying to bring women entrepreneurs into its activities, and in 1998/1999 it published a directory of women entrepreneurs in Pakistan that included information (name, address, contact numbers, type of business and products etc.) on more than 400 business women. The directory is divided into small (183), medium (216) and large (17) businesses.[27] Special training courses on export finance and export procedures have been delivered and a special handholding programme for women exporters has been designed. Women entrepreneurs and NGOs took part in a three-day exhibition called WEXNET 2001 which was organized by EPB at the Karachi Expo Centre in August 2001.

First Women's Bank Limited (FWBL)

The FWBL was established in 1989 as a nationalized commercial bank to cater solely to the financial needs of women entrepreneurs. Its mandate was to improve the socio-economic status of women in both urban and rural areas by creating opportunities for their development through enhanced economic participation. In a way it is designed to serve the duel objectives of a commercial bank and a development finance institution. The services offered by the Bank are:

♦ loans on easy terms for women entrepreneurs;
♦ advisory and consultancy services for investment;
♦ identification of agricultural and industrial projects for potential women entrepreneurs;
♦ training in technical and managerial skills;
♦ market development for the products of women entrepreneurs;
♦ promoting and sponsoring displays of clients' products in national and international exhibitions.[28]

The FWBL has 38 branches all over Pakistan and a head office in Karachi.[29] The Bank launched a small loan facility for women from low-income groups with an initial allocation of Rs. 30 million from the MoWD. Under this scheme women could borrow up to Rs. 25,000 (approximately US $ 400) by using a group guarantee, NGO warranty or personal surety from two government officials. Approximately 11,000 women have benefited from the small loan schemes in the last 10 years.[30] The Bank set up a Regional Development and Training Institute (RDTI) in Islamabad in 1995, and then in Lahore and Karachi. These training institutes were later re-named as business centres. FWBL has trained 3,093 women in different trades so far through these centres.[31] Under its policy of privatizing the national banks the Government planned to sell the FWBL, but the latest information (as at April 2002) indicates that the Bank has been removed from the privatization list.

---

[27] The categories are defined on the basis of production and marketing as follows: Large-scale is defined as businesses using specialized machinery which sell their products in the large national or international market; medium-scale refers to businesses using basic machinery that produce goods mainly for the national market; small businesses are household producers catering to wholesale buyers or small local markets.
[28] FWBL; *First in concept, second to none* (Pamphlet of FWBL).
[29] First Women Bank Limited; *Annual Report 2000*.
[30] *Study of FWBL and recommended JICA assistance to FWBL*: A study by JICA, Pakistan 1999.
[31] *Vision to develop support and empower the corporate women*, Draft paper by the FWBL, Dec. 2001.

10

1.3.3 Women's fora and other networking organizations

Women's support organizations mushroomed in Pakistan during the 1990s and most of these organizations are in the philanthropic sector. Those related to economic empowerment of women are confined to offering micro-credit and supporting subsistence activities. A few support commercial business but they have very limited outreach. The Pakistan Association of Women Entrepreneurs (PAWE) is one of these and was registered as a non-governmental organization (NGO) in 1985. Ms. Salma Ahmed, a leading entrepreneur from Karachi, has been the main driving force behind this organization; she has recently been succeeded by Ms. Zeenat Saeed, another eminent businesswomen from Karachi. PAWE is a member of the governing body of the World Assembly of Small and Medium Enterprises (WASME) and is affiliated to the Economic and Social Council of the UN (ECOSOC). PAWE has carried out various activities in urban areas, especially in Karachi, but there is little history of institutional undertakings except for representing the interests of women entrepreneurs at international fora.

The Association of Business, Professional and Agricultural Women is another organization in Karachi that engages in multiple activities to facilitate social harmony, and to promote an exchange of views and greater interaction amongst women. It has also identified business areas and prepared some pre-feasibility reports for enterprise creation. The Pakistan Federation of Business and Professional Women is yet another organization in Karachi engaged in similar activities. The Women Entrepreneurs Society (WES) is a tiny organization in Lahore with no significant activity.

The Federation of Pakistan Chamber of Commerce and Industry (FPCCI), Karachi also has a women's section, although the Karachi Chamber of Commerce and Industry (KCCI) does not have one. The women entrepreneurs' committee of the Lahore Chamber of Commerce and Industry is more organized and is preparing to arrange some concrete activities for the women entrepreneurs.

1.3.4 Employers' Federation of Pakistan (EFP)

The Employers' Federation of Pakistan, the national body of employers in Pakistan, is conscious of its responsibilities to encourage women into economic activities so as to enable them to contribute to national economic development. Part of this responsibility has been addressed through various project initiatives with the aim of supporting women's entrepreneurship development activities. EFP took the initiative and started a number of programmes to raise awareness among women through seminars, with the active assistance of the ILO and a number of donor agencies, like the World Bank, NORAD, etc. Since 1992, EFP has undertaken a number of action-oriented programmes in support of small enterprise development for women, such as:

- A seminar on the role of women in the national economy, and workshops on women's entrepreneurship development;
- Entrepreneurship training for women: a number of 2-day and 3-day workshops were held in different parts of the country;
- Awareness raising to promote women in economic activities;
- Workshops on the ILO's Start Your Business (SYB) and Improve Your Business (IYB) targeting women entrepreneurs, especially rural women entrepreneurs;
- Preparation of 16 feasibility reports on business opportunities for women that could be started with a small investment and a small outlay;
- In order to multiply the efforts initiated by EFP at the community-level, Training Of Trainers programmes were organized for educated women to be trained as trainers so that they could provide advisory and training services in the local communities. For this purpose, the ILO-SAAT Trainer's Manual titled, "Entrepreneurship Development for Women" was translated and printed in Urdu and widely circulated;

- Linkages have been developed by EFP with other agencies like the Aga Khan Rural Support Programme, Asia Foundation, Support for Entrepreneurship Programmes, etc. for the provision of credit and training facilities to women entrepreneurs;
- Plans for the establishment of an Advisory Cell for Women (ACW) were developed by EFP and the ILO to provide services to women and women entrepreneurs regarding entrepreneurship development, as well as career counselling and monitoring activities – the implementation of this proposal is still a priority item for the EFP;
- An EFP project implemented in collaboration with the Modern Institute of Secretarial Sciences (MISS) has trained more than 250 women in secretarial skills and computer operations. The majority of the trainees were placed in regular employment or obtained further on-the-job training with member organizations of the Federation.
- In 1996, the ILO-SAAT and experts in Islamabad developed for the EFP a project proposal entitled "Women's Employment - Strengthening Policy Planning, Co-ordination and Monitoring" for the EFP.
- The establishment of the Skills Development with the assistance of the ILO, World Bank and Employers' Federation has benefited many women to be able to access vocational training programmes which are demand-oriented and cost-effective. After attending the training courses, several women participants were gainfully occupied either through wage or self-employment.
- Several new programmes on IT and other vocational skills have been designed for implementation in the future. The establishment of a Skills Development Fund with the support of employers to fund women trainees who are unable to meet the cost of training programmes is another development exclusively addressing the needs of women for economic empowerment. In addition to the cost of training, small business loans to enable trainees to start their own businesses are being contemplated for those who need this financial support.
- Other activities that are being undertaken by EFP are career counselling and employment awareness programmes for students at the school/college levels, and workshops/seminars on technical and vocational training programmes for women.
- The ILO/Japan inter-country Project on Employment Promotion (PEP) generated employment for approximately 3,300 women, mainly through self-employment by starting micro-enterprises;
- The Dutch-funded ILO Project on Training and Employment for Rural Women (TERW) in the North-West Frontier Province aimed at income-generation, group formation, and provision of literacy and numeracy skills for women.

The EFP continues to see itself having an important role in supporting women entrepreneurs and welcoming them into the organizational framework of the Federation.

PART II

2.   Survey of 150 women entrepreneurs

2.1   Survey framework

The second part of this report consists of the results of a field survey based on a sample of 150 women entrepreneurs in Lahore and the twin cities of Rawalpindi and Islamabad. A team of female interviewers carried out the survey using a questionnaire (see Appendix F) to collect primary information. The instrument was designed to elicit extensive data on the women, their businesses and operating environments.

2.1.1   Definition of a woman entrepreneur for survey purposes

The working definition of a woman entrepreneur was very carefully framed after a series of consultations with officials from the International Labour Organization (ILO) in Islamabad, New Delhi and Geneva. The lower end of the business spectrum represented by subsistence enterprises was screened out in order to focus the survey on those enterprises which have potential for growth and upgrading. Three types of qualifying question regarding ownership, number of employees and business premises were included at the beginning to eliminate subsistence and household businesses. The first question on ownership made sure that the interviewee owns or manages, or has a majority share in the business. It was decided to include in the survey only those businesses that had five or more employees, and the second question ascertained that point. The third question was aimed at excluding household businesses from the survey. Only enterprises operating from dedicated premises (owned or rented) were selected.

2.1.2   Sampling frame

There is no readily available sampling frame for choosing a statistical sample of women entrepreneurs in Pakistan, nor even for small and medium enterprises. The Federal Bureau of Statistics (FBS) has recently started the first economic census of Pakistan, which is expected to provide the necessary frame for future surveys, but this is not likely to happen before 2004. The Survey of Small and Household Manufacturing Industries (SHMI 1996/97) and the Census of Manufacturing Industries (CMI 1996/97) were considered inadequate for our purposes. The SHMI includes household business, which was excluded from our survey, while the CMI excludes services and trade sectors, which were an integral part of this study.

2.1.3   Sample composition

The sample was stratified according to geographical location, size of enterprise and sector of operation (see Table 2). A brief description of each of these factors is given below.

Geographical location: The survey was carried out in Lahore, Rawalpindi and Islamabad Capital Territory (ICT).[32] Rawalpindi and ICT were surveyed together as they are twin cities; the sample distribution was made even by interviewing 75 women in Lahore and 75 in Rawalpindi/ICT.

---

[32] Lahore and Rawalpindi are big cities in Punjab province, accounting for more than half the national population. The selection of cities was deliberated at length with ILO as initially it was envisaged to distribute the whole sample in different administrative units of the Government of Pakistan. This included the four provinces, ICT, FATA, PATA, Azad Kashmir and FANA. A further distribution of the sample into micro, small and medium enterprises would have diluted each sub-set to only five women. Finally, two big cities of Punjab were chosen because it is estimated that around 60 per cent of small and medium enterprises exist in this province.

Table 2: Overview of the composition of the sample of women entrepreneurs

	All	City		Size of enterprise			Kind of business		
		Lhzr	Isb	Micro	Small	Medium	Trade	Manufac-turing	Service
Total sample (Nos.)	150	75	75	78	58	14	29	40	81
Age group						Percentages			
20-39	49	45	52	56	43	29	41	38	57
40-49	31	37	25	26	40	29	31	43	26
50-59	15	13	17	13	16	29	24	13	14
60 above	3	3	3	1	2	14	3	8	-
No response	1	-	3	3	-	-	-	-	2
Less than 20 years	1	1	-	1	-	-	-	-	1
Total	*100*	*100*	*100*	*100*	*100*	*100*	*100*	*100*	*100*
Level of education									
Graduate-Vocational	43	49	37	42	41	57	45	50	40
Postgraduate	32	29	35	29	34	36	31	20	38
Secondary-Primary	22	20	24	24	22	7	21	28	20
No formal education	2	1	3	3	2	-	3	3	1
No response	1	-	1	1	-	-	-	-	1
Total	*100*	*100*	*100*	*100*	*100*	*100*	*100*	*100*	*100*
Marital status									
Married	75	79	71	73	72	93	90	80	67
Single	21	17	24	24	19	7	10	15	27
Divorced	4	4	4	3	7	-	-	5	5
Separated	1	-	1	-	2	-	-	-	1
Total	*100*	*100*	*100*	*100*	*100*	*100*	*100*	*100*	*100*
Family structure									
Nuclear family	59	65	53	53	64	79	62	63	57
Extended family	35	32	39	38	34	21	34	35	36
Alone	5	3	8	9	2	-	3	3	7
Total	*100*	*100*	*100*	*100*	*100*	*100*	*100*	*100*	*100*
Engagement prior to business									
Housewife	47	52	41	44	50	50	66	65	31
Employed	28	28	28	24	33	29	21	20	35
Student	21	19	23	28	14	7	7	13	30
Unemployed	2	-	4	3	-	7	3	-	2
Another business	2	1	3	1	2	7	3	-	2
No response	1	-	1	-	2	-	-	3	-
Total	*100*	*100*	*100*	*100*	*100*	*100*	*100*	*100*	*100*

14

Size of enterprise: Household and tiny enterprises were screened out. The survey, however, distinguished between micro, small and medium enterprises. An enterprise was defined as micro if it employed 5 to 9 workers, small for 10 to 35, and medium for 36 to 99 workers. At least ten women entrepreneurs from each category were included.

Allocation by sector: The sample was further divided into manufacturing, retail trade and services. There are approximately 400,000 small-scale manufacturing units, 600,000 service-sector units and one million retailers in Pakistan, making a total of approximately 2 million units.[33] It was agreed that a minimum of 25 women entrepreneurs would be included from each sector in the total sample.

2.1.4 Methodology

The survey was carried out using the snowballing technique for identifying respondents. The initial contacts were the most difficult to establish as there are very few resources that could be used for this purpose. The *Directory of Women Entrepreneurs* published by Export Promotion Board (EPB) and the respective Chambers of Commerce and Industry were the starting points. The women who were interviewed first were requested to provide the names and addresses of other women entrepreneurs who might take part in the survey.

2.1.5 Design of the survey instrument

The questionnaire was designed in accordance with guidance provided in the background concept paper prepared by the ILO (see appendix G). It was divided into four sections. The first section focused on the profile of women entrepreneurs. The second dealt with structural aspects of the enterprise and issues associated with the family and the enterprise. The third dealt exclusively with the business environment and included sub-sections on government policies, regulations and institutions, financial and non-financial services. The last section was designed to investigate social/cultural issues confronted by women entrepreneurs.[34]

The pilot testing consisted of interviews with four women entrepreneurs; these were conducted simultaneously in Lahore and Rawalpindi/ICT. Two of the subjects found that the questionnaire was very lengthy and that some questions in the business environment section were very technical. Two questions were eliminated, and others were rephrased. All four subjects, however, indicated that it would be worthwhile if the questionnaire was in Urdu and not in English. This was justified by the very low female literacy rate and poor understanding of English in general in Pakistan. The questionnaire was therefore translated into Urdu. Two training sessions were held for the interviewers in Lahore and Islamabad. A handbook was prepared for their guidance, explaining the rationale of the survey and clarifying certain questions. Lengthy questions were printed on cards to be shown to the interviewees to reduce the time needed for the questionnaire.

2.1.6 Problems faced during the survey

The material related to the field work had to be translated into Urdu, which was a lengthy and cumbersome process. In consultation with Gallup Pakistan, who have vast experience of

---

[33] *SMEDA Profile*, A brochure of SMEDA, Lahore.

[34] The first draft of the questionnaire was shared with Mr. Gerry Finnegan, Senior Specialist, Women's Entrepreneurship Development and Gender Equality (WEDGE), ILO, Geneva, Ms. Jyoti Tuladhar, Senior Gender Specialist, ILO SAAT in New Delhi, Ms. Samina Hassan, Programme Officer, ILO Islamabad, and Mr. Johannes Lokollo, Director, ILO Islamabad. Comments were also sought from Ms. Saadya Hamdani of the Royal Norwegian Embassy, Ms. Abida Aziz of the Asia Foundation, Ms. Samia Rauf, Consultant ADB, Pakistan, Ms. Musarrat Bashir of IUCN and Mr. Arshed Bhatti of the Planning Commission of Pakistan. The feedback was incorporated and a semi-final draft was circulated again. A final review of the questionnaire was made jointly with the ILO team before pilot testing.

carrying out opinion polls, the guidebook, question cards and questionnaire were practically re-written in Urdu.

Unfortunately, the survey coincided with the national income tax survey of the Government of Pakistan, which is carried out by the Central Bureau of Revenue (CBR). The national tax survey met with strong resistance in the form of boycotts, shutter-down strikes and angry demonstrations by the business community. The tax authorities were using military and para-military troops to carry out their survey. This had an adverse effect on our exercise. Most of the women entrepreneurs contacted thought that the government was playing another trick to complete its tax survey. An introductory letter was therefore sent to the women entrepreneurs before the telephone contact. A letter was also given to the interviewers guaranteeing confidentiality. Despite this it was still necessary to telephone more than once, and in some cases a prior courtesy call had to be made to persuade the women to agree to be interviewed.

As already mentioned, there are hardly any data on women entrepreneurs that could be used as a sampling frame. The *Directory of Women Entrepreneurs* published by the Export Promotion Bureau of the Government of Pakistan was the starting point but the majority of businesses included in this directory are in Karachi. The telephone numbers of some companies were either incorrect or they had changed. Lahore and Rawalpindi Chamber of Commerce were able to provide very few names and addresses, while the FWBL records were replete with tiny businesses that were outside the scope of this survey.

The introductory letter contained some background information about the project. It also stated that the interview was expected to take more than an hour but it was difficult to keep the entrepreneurs strictly engaged with the questionnaire. The multiple engagements of women entrepreneurs, such as picking up children from school, answering phone calls and receiving unexpected visitors (common in Pakistan) contributed to delays and many interviews had to be completed on another occasion. Almost a quarter of the interviews took more than one sitting.

The women entrepreneurs sometimes hesitated to answer certain questions and tried to buy time for consultation. This was more true of questions about who signs the legal documents, total investment in the business, monthly profits, etc. They normally sought the help of their male relatives who may or may not have attended the interview. The usual response to such questions was "Pooch kar bataoon gee — Let me consult and then I will tell".

It was difficult to recruit the survey team. Although Gallup Pakistan, with its rich experience in opinion polls was used to recruiting, the female interviewers were shy about talking to women entrepreneurs as it was field work and involved intra-city traveling. A vehicle was later arranged to facilitate travelling, but still the majority of prospective interviewers refused the job on the grounds that their families would not permit them to do such work. Four female graduates were finally recruited, trained and sent in pairs for pilot testing in Lahore as part of the first phase. All four declined to carry out the survey after pilot testing, despite the offer of very generous remuneration. They insisted that they would prefer an office job where a male relative could drop them in the morning and pick them up in the evening. The next team was a mix of two experienced female interviewers from the Gallup office and two new recruits. The same scheme worked in Rawalpindi, and the subsequent phase of the field survey remained manageable.

A training manual was prepared for the interviewers and joint training was planned for Lahore, but neither team would travel to the other city. Two training courses therefore had to be arranged, one in Lahore and the other in Rawalpindi/Islamabad.

The interviewers in Rawalpindi/ICT worked in pairs, as they felt more comfortable moving together. One pair requested that a male employee of Gallup should accompany them for some initial interviews.

16

The quality review of the field work was done in parallel but this still prolonged the task. The interviewers were carefully selected and most had Masters' degrees. They were briefed about the project and systematically trained to get answers but about 10 per cent of the questionnaires had to be returned after the quality review to expand or clarify the responses.[35]

Last but not least came the post-September 11 scenario. Almost every business in Pakistan was affected by the aftermath of the terrorist attacks in the United States and the subsequent events. Export orders were cancelled, freight was delayed and uncertainty prevailed. The whole business community, including women entrepreneurs, had to concentrate on solving their problems and had little time for interviews.

2.1.7 Project team

The names and titles of the project team are given in Appendix E and the final survey instrument appears in Appendix F.

2.2 Survey results

The questionnaire was divided into four major parts to obtain general and specific information related to the women entrepreneurs, their business and the business environment.

◆ Profile of the entrepreneur
◆ Profile of the enterprise
    a. General
    b. Business and the family
◆ Business environment
    c. Government policies, regulations and institutions
    d. Financial services
    e. Non-financial services
◆ Social/cultural influences

The questionnaire included structured and open-ended questions to elicit both quantitative and qualitative information. The sections below provide a description and analysis of the results.

2.2.1 Profile of the women entrepreneurs

Age: Forty-nine per cent of respondents were aged between 20-39 and 31 per cent were between 40-49. The probability of starting and running a business falls dramatically after the age of 50, dropping to 15 per cent for the age bracket 50-59 and to 3 per cent after 60. On the other hand, only one respondent was below the age of 20.

Children: The other significant finding is the below-average number of children of women entrepreneurs compared to other Pakistani women. Sixty-five per cent of respondents had only one or two children.[36]

Family context: The likelihood of a Pakistani woman being in business is greater if she lives in a nuclear family structure.[37] While the predominant mode in Pakistan is an extended family structure,[38] 59 per cent of the respondents were found to be living in a nuclear family. This would mean relatively less interaction with the older generation and less exposure to their

---

[35] A typical example would be that most women entrepreneurs wanted government help in their business but did not specify the kind of help. They indicated that the government should be responsive to their needs.

[36] The average household size in Pakistan is 6.6 according to the National Population and Housing Census of Pakistan 1998 published in 2000.

[37] Nuclear family denotes husband, wife and unmarried children.

[38] Nuclear family and other relatives.

social/cultural influence. Conventional wisdom would expect better mobility and improved chances of being in some economic activity, especially when coupled with better education.

Literacy and education: The literacy rate of women entrepreneurs and their close relatives is well above the national average. The female literacy rate is 32.6 per cent in Pakistan and 35.3 per cent in the province of Punjab.[39] Table 3 shows the educational attainment of respondents, 97 per cent of whom are literate.

Table 3: Educational levels of respondents and their close relations
(% of responses)

Level of education	Self	Mother	Father	Spouse*
Postgraduate	32	3	26	43
Graduate/vocational	43	12	37	39
Secondary/primary	22	52	26	14
Just literate	0	19	6	1
No formal education	2	12	5	1
No response	0	2	0	2

* The percentages in this column are not based upon all the respondents but only the married women (75 per cent)

Information regarding the level of education is revealing as it indicates that the majority of women entrepreneurs belonged to the upper tiers of graduates (43 per cent) and post-graduates (32 per cent). The educational levels of the respondents' mothers were generally lower than their fathers but they were still far above the national average. As most of the women entrepreneurs were married (75 per cent) the educational level of their husbands was also ascertained. This was also significantly above the national average, 82 per cent being in the graduate/vocational or post-graduate categories. This shows that an educated woman with an educated family background is much more likely than an average Pakistani woman to start or run a business.

Training and work experience: More than half of the respondents had attained a professional diploma, certificate or technical training (nursing, make-up, beautician etc.) before going into business. Forty-three per cent had substantial work experience, 21 per cent had little experience, and 35 per cent started from scratch. Chart 5 shows that 47 per cent of women entrepreneurs were housewives before starting business, 28 per cent were employed in different capacities with different organizations, and 21 per cent were students.

---

[39] *Pakistan Statistical Yearbook 2001*, Federal Bureau of Statistics, Statistics Division, Government of Pakistan, Islamabad. N.B. "Literacy" is defined as the ability to read and write one's name. It does not relate to formal schooling.

Chart 5: Previous occupation

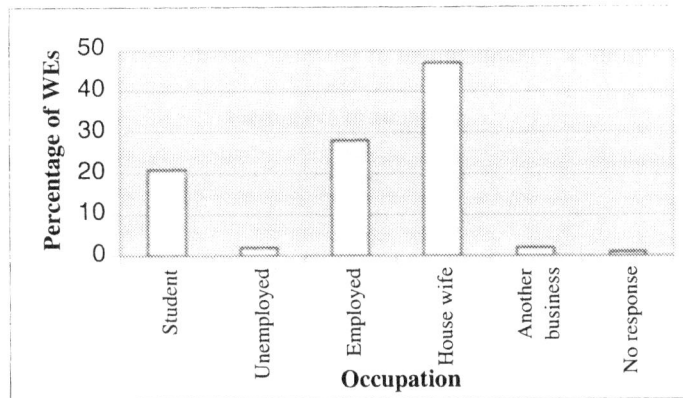

Management style: Fifty-nine per cent of women entrepreneurs use a hierarchical management style while 39 per cent believe in a consensus-based approach. A majority of 77 per cent believe that this is more effective; 14 per cent say that it suits the culture and 7 per cent are convinced that it is more productive. However, the questionnaire invited only a limited range of responses to this topic, and the information obtained would require closer investigation.

Chart 6: Management styles of women entrepreneurs

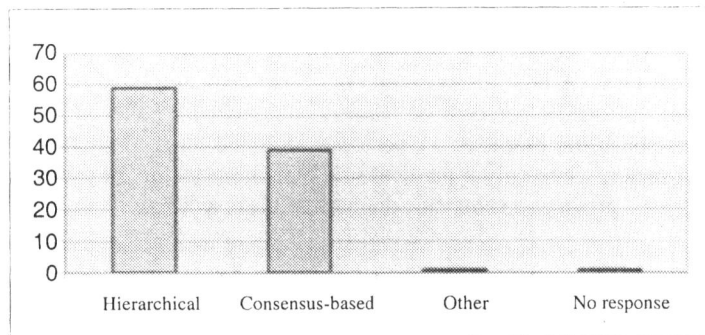

Computer literacy: The computer skills of women entrepreneurs are also better than average: 31 per cent felt confident that they could compose a letter on a personal computer; 37 per cent could use e-mail and Internet, 11 per cent were able to use spreadsheets and prepare power point presentations while the remaining 8 per cent had even better skills than all those mentioned above. These figures are also above the national average, according to which 84 per cent of the computer literate population in Pakistan are men.[40]

START-UP

Start-up and ownership: Concerning the pattern of start-up, the majority of respondents claimed that they established the business by themselves.[41] Nine per cent inherited their business. Further examination revealed that male family members set up 67 per cent of "already established" business: 21 per cent were established jointly by the woman entrepreneur and the family — 81 per

---

[40] *National IT Survey Top Line Results* conducted by Gallup Pakistan for IT and Telecommunication Division, Ministry of Science of Technology, Islamabad.

[41] Section 2.2.2 highlights the types of business that women entrepreneurs are generally in. The majority are in conventional women-focused activities such as beauty parlours, nursing clinics, schools etc. that do not involve much male interaction.

cent of whom sought the help of their male relatives to establish the business. Hence the dependence on male relatives remains strong for those who seek family help.

Table 4: Establishment of business: Sex-disaggregated

	Percent of responses	Female	Male
Already established by family	9		
(Sex disaggregated)		3	6
Myself	64		
Myself and my family	21		
(Sex disaggregated)		4	17
Myself and my friends	5		
Somebody else	1		

Motivation to start business: What motivates women in Pakistan to start a business? This was a multiple response question addressed only to respondents who had started a business by themselves. Seventy-six per cent mentioned economic reasons that varied between the "urge to make money" to "financial crisis in the family". The other significant reasons were continuation of hobby (53 per cent), productive occupation (47 per cent), desire for recognition and economic independence (24 per cent) and philanthropy (9 per cent). The predominance of economic reasons is understandable when we relate it to the difficulties experienced by the Pakistan economy since the 1990s.[42]

Factors contributing to start-up: The survey attempted to identify any gender-specific factors that were helpful in business start-up, and any problems that may have hindered the establishment of business. A high response rate of 75 per cent suggested family help as the most important enabling factor; 30 per cent of women entrepreneurs believed that their own skills helped them to establish the business; 11 per cent attributed their commitment to developing a hobby as a major factor, while only 3 per cent said that cheap factors of production (FOP) was a helping factor. Chart 7 provides a schematic diagram of the responses.

---

[42] The economic difficulties of the 1990s have exacerbated poverty in Pakistan. The spiral of internal instabilities and external shocks starting in 1988 deteriorated with the natural calamities of 1992/93. A severe economic crisis has plagued the country since then. Deflationary Structural Adjustment (SA) Policies have compounded the difficulties. Slow economic growth, drastic cuts in the Public Sector Development Programme (PSDP), stagnant investment, downsizing in government departments, the ban on new positions and a huge inflow of returning expatriates are some contributing factors in the rise of unemployment and poverty. There are no new jobs to accommodate the labour force which is growing at 3.3 per cent annually. The government, in a desperate attempt to collect revenues, has been increasing indirect taxes that now comprise 80 per cent of the total tax revenue. Privatization of the public sector corporations under the structural adjustment programme has resulted in high prices for the privatized services and a rise in utility bills that is pushing more people into poverty. Income poverty reaching the lowest ebb of 20 per cent in 1990 had risen to 30 per cent in 1995.

Chart 7: Helpful factors in business start-up

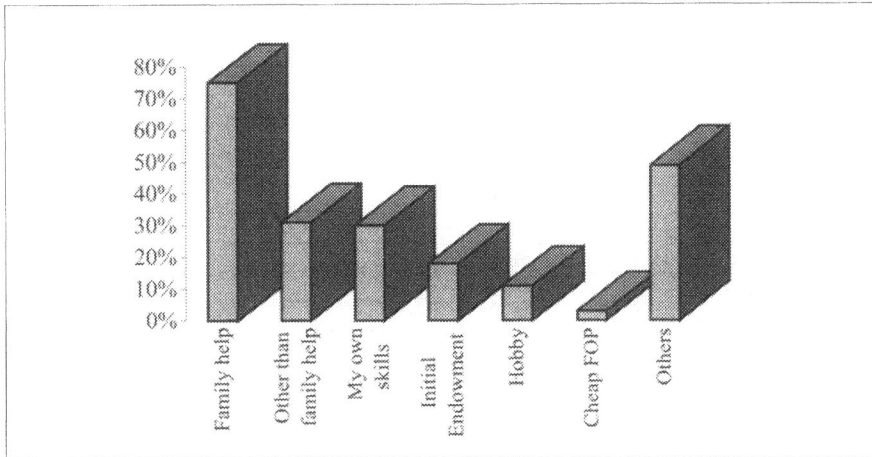

Problems and barriers at start-up: The surveyed sample was also asked to indicate three major problems faced during the start-up phase. The various problems indicated by the respondents were grouped into nine categories. Table 5 provides a complete picture of the results, for which titles have been assigned to the clusters of answers, and sub-titles show the actual problems mentioned by the women entrepreneurs.

Table 5: Retarding factors in business start-up

	Percentage of responses
Gender biases	**51**
People were not cooperative towards women	12
Hostile attitude of men towards working women	11
Dealing with men is difficult	7
Labour attitude/dealing with male workers	7
Male-dominated society	4
Non-professional behaviour of male entrepreneurs	4
Credit recovery was a problem (weak bargaining position)	3
No one to guide/support females	2
No contact in the male-dominated society	1
Marketing	**28**
It was a problem to attract customers	7
No sale point was available	7
Unfavourable market behaviour	4
Finding market was a difficult job	3
No outlet for marketing	1
Family/social	**26**
Non-supportive family	9
Household responsibility/engagements	7
Time distribution between family and business	6
Children were neglected	4
Finance	**24**
Lack of finance	24
Related to government	**16**
Government departments were not cooperative	7
Government policies/ regulations were stringent	2
Bribery	1
To get registered was a big problem	1
Lack of government facilities	2
Police harassment	1
Electricity connection	1
To get national tax number was a problem	1
Mobility	**6**
Transport problems	6
Others	**28**
Convincing people	9
Raw material was not easily available	7
Expenses were higher than income	3
Lack of knowledge	1
I was not experienced enough to run a business	2
Incurred high costs on purchasing machinery/equipment	1
Felt difficulties to fulfill big orders	1
Labour was not easily available	4
Did not face any problems	**14**
No response	**1**

2.2.2 Profile of the enterprise

Scale: Women's enterprises were defined in terms of employment and divided into micro (5-9 workers), small (10-35) and medium (36-99) enterprises. Fifty-two per cent of the surveyed sample were in the first group, 39 per cent in the second and 9 per cent in the third. Nineteen per cent were engaged in trading, 27 per cent in manufacturing and 54 per cent were in the service sector.[43] Given the range of social and cultural barriers facing women in Pakistan, this might be seen as a pragmatic entrepreneurial response to their restricted participation in the economy.

Sector: A further probe reflected the conservative attitude of women entrepreneurs where most women (135 per cent – this figure is based on the women entrepreneurs having more than one business) were engaged in traditional business and a tiny minority (7 per cent) were in non-traditional business.[44] The main business areas that attract their interest seem to be those which involve minimal interaction with men. Chart 8 shows the main areas of engagement.

Chart 8: Women's businesses by sector

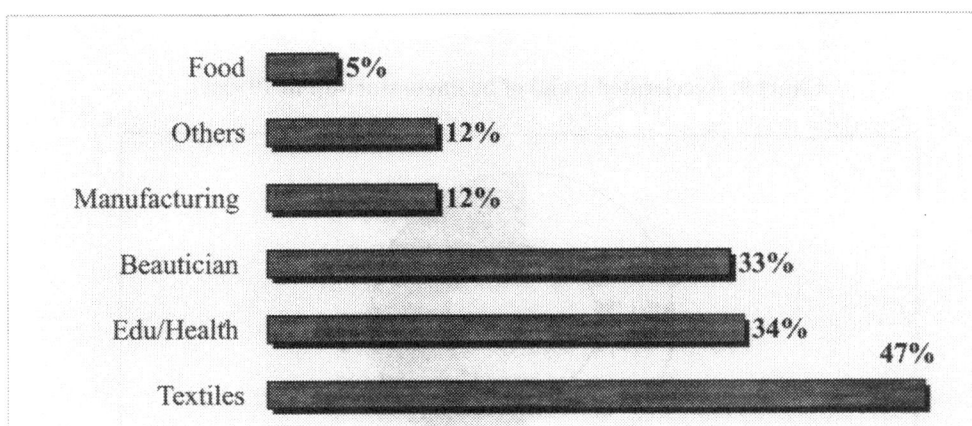

Textiles and apparel is the prime area of activity. The full range includes ready-made garments, bridal wear, embroidery, stitching, lace-making and ladies' boutiques; education and health services ranging from running tuition centres to secondary schools and clinics; beautician covering all activities related to beauty and health; food business comprising of bakeries and restaurants, while manufacturing generally includes making small items like lamp-shades, plastic toys and buttons.

Number and sex of workers: Another revealing finding of the survey was that women entrepreneurs employ more women workers than their male counterparts. Table 6 shows the average numbers employed by women entrepreneurs. The survey results indicate an average of eight full-time women employees (53 per cent) in each business as compared to seven men. This means that there is a more balanced labour force in enterprises owned by women. The average ratio in reporting factories in Pakistan is around 5:95 which indicates a strong negative bias against women in the labour force.[45] Hence the results indicate that the probability of employment for women is very much higher in an enterprise owned by a woman than in a male-owned business. The average percentage for part-time employees in the table is similar. Another

---

[43] Respondents were asked to identify themselves in one category of business.

[44] The percentage is more than 100 as many women entrepreneurs are engaged in more than one business and each discrete stream is considered as a separate business.

[45] The calculation is based on figures given in Table 3.15 of *Average daily number of factory workers in reporting factories by sex*, page 94 of Pakistan Statistical Yearbook 2001, Federal Bureau of Statistics, Government of Pakistan, Islamabad April, 2001.

interesting finding is the dominance of male family members in the paid category compared to female relatives who dominate in the unpaid category.

Table 6: Pattern of employees

Type of employees	Women (average of % of responses)	Men (average of % of responses)
Full-time	8	7
Part-time	5	5
Paid family member	2	5
Unpaid family member	2	1

Age of business: Answers to the question on "year of establishment of business" reflect an increasing trend towards women's business start-up. Chart 6 shows that only 23 per cent of businesses in the survey sample were established before 1990 (the oldest was established in 1951); 27 per cent were started between 1991 to 1995 while 50 per cent have been established since 1996.

Chart 9: Accelerated trend of business start-up in 1990s

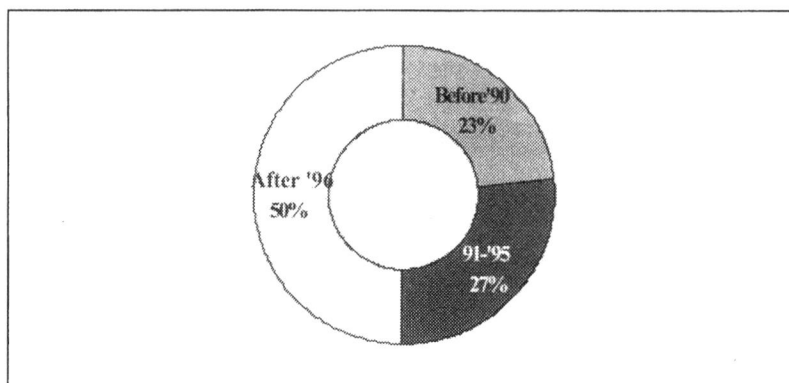

Location and ownership of premises: Some other manifestations of the conservative approach of women entrepreneurs are the concentration of business operations in the same city and the preponderance of sole proprietorship in terms of legal status. Once again, this can be seen as a pragmatic entrepreneurial response given women's limited mobility in society. Ninety-seven per cent of the businesses exist and operate in the same city. There was an almost equal split between owned and rented premises: 47 per cent of respondents were operating in their own premises (belonging to them or a member of the family) while 53 per cent were in rented accommodation.

Legal structure: Eighty-two per cent have the legal status of a sole proprietorship, which is the simplest form of business organization requiring no legal formalities.[46] Thirteen per cent of the sample surveyed operate as registered partnerships, and none was incorporated as a private company or a public listed company. It is interesting to note that the proportion of partnerships in the businesses owned by women is twice the national average. The Integrated Survey of Services and Manufacturing Industries (ISSMI) 1991/92 shows that 92.5 per cent of small businesses in Pakistan are sole proprietorships and 5.9 per cent are partnerships.[47]

---

[46] The majority of micro and small businesses in Pakistan operate as sole proprietors. This is the simplest form of legal business with no regulatory requirements. This significantly reduces the interaction between the government and the entrepreneur, although it does not provide tax exemption.
[47] ISSMI was carried out in 1991/92 by the Federal Bureau of Statistics, Government of Pakistan but was not published.

Chart 10: Legal forms of women's businesses

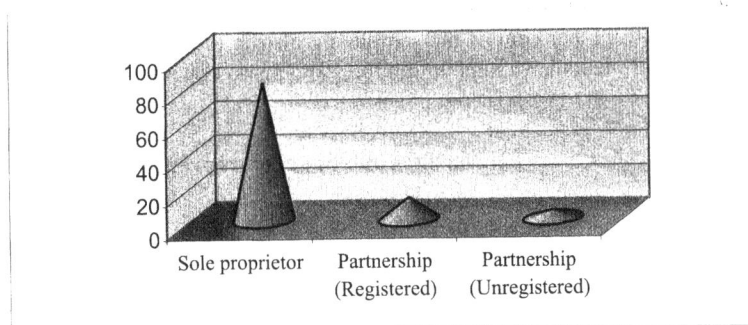

MARKETING

Importance of Marketing: Marketing is one of the most important aspects of business and it impacts considerably on the entrepreneur's standing in the supply chain. Consequently, it was investigated in some detail. The findings reported below show that the dominant mode of marketing among businesswomen is relationship-based: 38 per cent resort to personal contacts; 24 per cent market through exhibitions and social gatherings and 10 per cent use intermediaries. Others (26 per cent) referred to telephone orders.[48]

Chart 11: Mode of marketing

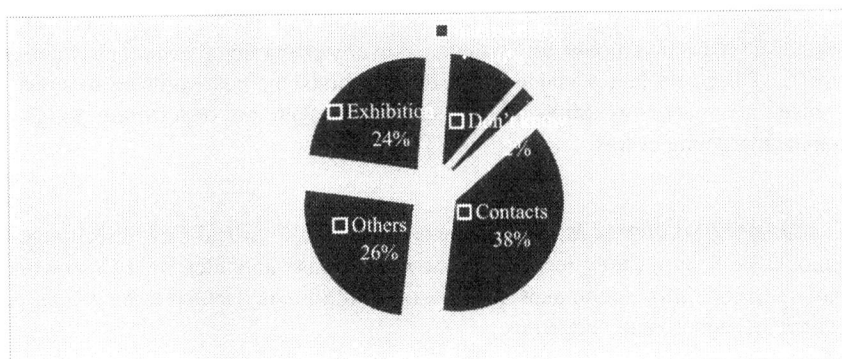

Getting orders: Sixty-five per cent of women entrepreneurs take orders themselves while 23 per cent receive orders through their marketing staff. Ninety-five per cent of businesswomen do not feel any constraint in getting orders, and 93 per cent provide a delivery service. As mentioned earlier, most of the respondents are in businesses that do not require extensive male interaction, so that marketing is not a daunting challenge. However, they employ marketing staff and the gender composition of the marketing personnel is shown in table 7.

Table 7: Male and female marketing staff

Male	Female	Both	No response
37%	26%	14%	23%
Base is 23% (n = 34))			

---

[48] The respondents running beauty parlours, health and beauty clinics said that their customers normally contacted them by telephone; they also marketed their services by making phone calls to contacts.

Location of market: Chart 12 shows that 79 per cent of respondents deal in the local markets; 13 per cent sell their products/services in the regional markets, 7 per cent extend to national markets while 11 per cent of the sample are also in the export category.[49] Sixty-five per cent of women entrepreneurs have kept within the same markets while the rest have explored other outlets.

Chart 12: Markets of women entrepreneurs

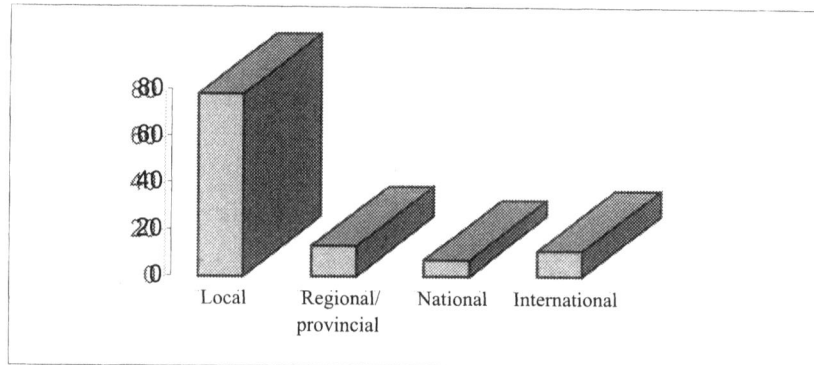

Marketing trends and strategies: A question was asked about marketing trends: 37 per cent wanted to explore further in the local markets; 33 per cent were content and wanted to remain in their existing markets; 9 per cent indicated regional markets, 7 per cent intended to look for national markets and 19 per cent were interested in international markets. In relation to the marketing strategies adopted, only 9 per cent of women entrepreneurs had a web-site to promote their business. Sixty per cent had not participated in any promotional event or exhibition in the last three years; 33 per cent had attended national exhibitions; 11 had exposure to some networking event related to marketing while 11 per cent had taken an opportunity to go abroad for international marketing events.

Marketing constraints: Respondents were asked to indicate three major marketing constraints; table 8 shows their responses. The major constraints identified (interaction and weak bargaining position, information gaps and lack of mobility) are deemed to be greater problems for women than for men in many countries.

Table 8: Marketing constraints[50]

No problem/constraints	48%
Interaction/weak bargaining position	34%
Information gaps	27%
General constraints	17%
Mobility	7%
Don't know	2%
No response	1%

The question of marketing constraints was further probed among the respondents who experienced problems (7 per cent). It transpired that 120 per cent of their problems were gender-related while 20 per cent were of a common nature. Note: Multiple responses were received.

---

[49] 11 per cent is a rather high percentage of women entrepreneurs to be in the export business. There could be a strong positive bias for the exporters, as random sampling was not done. Instead the Directory of Women Entrepreneurs published by the Export Promotion Bureau was used as a starting point, and the snowballing technique was used to identify further respondents.

[50] The cumulative percentages exceed 100 per cent as some respondents marked more than one factor in the multiple response questions.

26

TECHNOLOGY

Use of Technology: The survey found that the technological level of women's enterprises was very low.[51] Half of the surveyed sample had made no technology improvement in their business in the last year; 18 per cent had made marginal additions, 27 per cent had made moderate improvements while 5 per cent claimed to have made a substantial input. Those respondents who had made improvements were asked to give details (see table 9).

Table 9: Technology improvement in the business

Technology improvement	Percentage of responses
New computers	37
Advanced equipment	33
Purchased massage machines	15
Embroidery machine	8
Mobile phones	4
Lap-top computers	4
Internet marketing	4
Steam machine	4
Air conditioners	4

Type of Technology needed: One question was designed to ascertain the kind of technology that could be useful for women's business: 49 per cent of respondents placed information and communication technologies (ICT) at the top. It is also interesting to note that 15 per cent wanted to add technologies that could be helpful for the education of their family, especially the children. This highlights an important convergence between women's productive and reproductive roles, and indicates practical ways in which women entrepreneurs balance the two.

Chart 13: Type of technology helpful for business

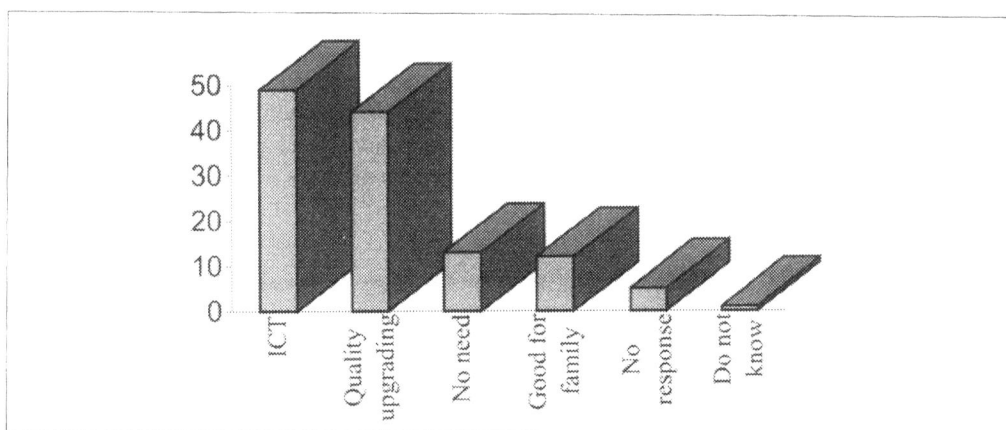

Awareness of technology and trade institutions: Two questions were asked to ascertain the respondents' knowledge of the technology-related national institutions, as well as their understanding of the World Trade Organization (WTO) and Pakistan's accession to it.

Thirty per cent knew about the Pakistan Council for Scientific and Industrial Research (PCSIR); 5 per cent were aware of the Scientific and Technological Development Corporation

---

[51] This is consistent with the universal trend as technology is generally considered a male domain.

(STEDEC); 9 per cent knew of the Pakistan Industrial and Technical Assistance Center (PITAC); 5 per cent knew of the National Productivity Organization (NPO); 25 per cent knew about the Punjab Vocational Training Council (PVTC) and 21 per cent about the Technical Education and Vocational Training Authority (TEVTA). This finding also highlights a gap in the supply and demand for technology. On the supply side, many technology support service providers are gender blind and make no special effort to include and assist women. On the demand side, many women are not aware that such support is available, or they view it as a "man's world". This situation serves to reinforce women's low awareness of and poor access to technology support, and contributes to women entrepreneurs' continued presence in low investment, low technology enterprises operating at the economic margins.

Pakistan and the WTO: Regarding Pakistan's accession to WTO, 53 per cent of women entrepreneurs had no idea how this was going to affect their business. Twenty-six per cent of respondents expected that it would affect their business favourably; 18 per cent believed that it would have a moderate effect on their business; 2 per cent thought it could have extremely bad consequences, while 1 per cent did not respond.

Table 10: Perceptions about Pakistan's accession to WTO

Will affect my business	Percentage response
Favourably	26
Moderately	18
Drastically	2
Have no idea	53
No response	1

OVERALL BUSINESS PERFORMANCE AND PROSPECTS

Business performance - Past, present and future: When asked about their business experience of the last year and expectations about future growth, the majority of women entrepreneurs responded positively: 61 per cent reported that their business had experienced normal growth during the previous year; 11 per cent reported phenomenal growth; 17 per cent remained stable; 9 per cent suffered negative growth and 2 per cent had suffered a drastic decline in their business. Ninety-two per cent intend to continue and expand their business. They were asked to explain how they intend to expand: table 11 shows their plans.

Table 11: Plans for future expansion (multiple response question)

	Percentage of responses
Expand/improve the business	69
Make new investments in the business	42
Increase the number of workers	27
Expand the range of products/services	26
Don't know	11
Other	3

Hopes and aspirations: Eighty-three per cent of respondents said they wanted their business to grow, while 16 per cent wished to retain the level they had already achieved.

Future expectations: Responding to another question 42 per cent said they expected their business to perform very well in the next 3 years; 40 per cent anticipated good performance, while 16 per cent foresaw moderate achievement.

Influence of business environment: An overall perception about the business environment was investigated by posing nine questions and asking for the respondents' opinions on a 5-point rating scale. Table 12 provides the detailed responses.

Table 12: Perceptions of the business environment

	Percentage of responses						
	+2 Strongly agree	+1 Agree	0 Can't say anything	-1 Disagree	-2 Strongly disagree	Cumulative Value	Rank
The overall environment for women entrepreneurs is good	25	52	5	6	12	+72	(5)
Family and social commitments are growing	56	21	17	5	1	+126	(1)
Government support to women entrepreneurs is increasing	4	17	36	15	28	-46	(8)
The costs of running a business are increasing	53	21	12	11	3	+110	(2)
Access to finance/credit for women entrepreneurs is increasing	1	14	38	13	34	-63	(9)
Access to women business support networks is increasing	3	39	19	13	26	-24	(7)
Market for women entrepreneurs is expanding	24	47	8	13	9	+64	(6)
Business know how of women entrepreneurs is increasing	29	46	12	9	5	+85	(4)
Technical skills of women entrepreneurs are increasing	32	43	13	9	3	+92	(3)

Factors influencing business growth: Using multiple responses the interviewees were asked to indicate the most important factors that could help their business grow: 49 per cent marked less and better government; 47 per cent desired business development services, and 46 per cent asked for concessionary finance[52].

Perceived barriers to growth: Answering another multiple response question on the significant barriers to business growth, many respondents (45 per cent) indicated gender-specific social barriers, 41 per cent blamed the government for creating an unhealthy business environment, 31 per cent mentioned lack of finance while 20 per cent indicated the absence of adequate business development services.

2.2.3 The business environment

GOVERNMENT POLICIES, REGULATIONS AND INSTITUTIONS

Policy environment: The opinions of women entrepreneurs are divided on the present policy environment in Pakistan: 26 per cent are of the view that the present environment discriminates against them; 19 per cent think otherwise. As many as 35 per cent think that it is

---

[52] The cumulative percentages exceed 100 per cent as some respondents marked more than one factor in the multiple response questions.

neutral and 21 per cent have no opinion about it. The survey revealed that more than half of the women entrepreneurs did not know about government policies related to investment, trade and export promotion, income and sales tax, concessionary finance and labour regulations. None of the respondents knew about the Statutory Regulatory Ordinances (SROs) that are issued by the Central Bureau of Revenue (CBR) for business and tariff concessions. Table 13 provides details of the responses.

Table 13: Knowledge of government policies

	Percentage of responses		
	Yes	No	No response
Policies of the Board of Investment that provide incentives for new and existing investments	34	65	1
Policies of the Ministry of Commerce and Industry for trade and export promotion	41	58	1
Policies of the Ministry of Finance (income and sales tax concessions)	53	47	-
Policies of the State Bank of Pakistan for concession in loans	35	65	-
SROs issued by the Central Bureau of Revenue for tariff concessions	0	100	-
Policies of the Ministry of Labour that entail labour-related regulations	35	65	-

Taxation and regulations: Taxation regulations were singled out by 71 per of respondents as the most troublesome area of government regulations to comply with; 14 per cent mentioned licensing; 10 per cent indicated trade regulations; 5 per cent referred to business regulations, while 3 per cent found that labour laws were the most difficult to observe.

Negative factors affecting women's business: One-third of the women entrepreneurs thought that lack of adequate financing facilities was a major factor that had negatively affected their business in the recent past. Others referred to the regulatory environment (23 per cent), law and order (18 per cent), lack of BDS (10 per cent), and economic slowdown (9 per cent).

Supportive policy suggestions: The respondents were asked to suggest policy inputs that the government should incorporate to promote women entrepreneurs. The majority regarded "over-government" as a major constraint in running their business. Others suggested financing, BDS and networking opportunities as valid options. There was a large number of references to gender-related factors. Table 14 provides a complete picture with titles and sub-titles.

Table 14: Suggested changes in government policies
(percentage of responses)

Less and easy government (This was an open-ended question. Some specific responses are shown below)	**64**
Policies should be in favour of women entrepreneurs	15
Loans-sanctioning procedure must be simplified	12
Separate policies for women entrepreneurs should be brought in	12
Policies should be stable	6
Reduce taxes	4
There should be proper implementation of policies	3
Government officials should be ethically trained	2
Quota system should be changed	1
Income tax should decrease to a normal limit	1
Sales tax should decrease to a normal limit	1
There should not be red tape	1
Less documentation and easy paper work	1
All policies should be fair/practical	1
Financing (Some specific responses are shown below)	**29**
Loans should be provided to women entrepreneurs at low interest rates	18
Finance policies should be favourable	5
Interest-free loans should be provided to women entrepreneur	3
Easy access to banks for loans/funds	3
There should not be collateral restrictions for women entrepreneurs	1
Business Development Services (Some specific responses are shown below)	**19**
More technical training centres should be established	8
There should be exhibitions for women only and separate markets	4
Government should provide assistance in marketing to women entrepreneurs	3
Proper outlets should be provided to women	2
Policies for special training of women entrepreneurs	1
There should be proper technical schools where women can have training	1
Women should be trained in legal matters	1
Information/networking fora (Some specific responses are shown below)	**17**
Information fora for women entrepreneurs regarding government policies	9
Government should develop women's network to promote women entrepreneur	5
There should be a club for skilled women, where they can get all facilities	3
Others (Some specific responses are shown below)	**23**
Policies regarding social protection to women entrepreneurs should be formulated	
Women should be appointed at govt. offices to handle all matters regarding women entrepreneurs	5
Payment recovery system should be developed	1
Government policies cannot be changed	2
Don't know	**3**
No response	**1**

FINANCIAL SERVICES

Bank accounts: Eighteen per cent of the women running a formal business did not have a personal bank account. Fifty-five per cent of the account holders had a separate account for the business while 44 per cent did not differentiate between their personal account and their business bank account.

Start-up capital: The predominant source of start-up capital for business was reported as personal savings (73 per cent); informal sources were in second position at 19 per cent.[53] Only 4 per cent of respondents had access to formal sources of credit (see chart 17). The survey did not reveal how many respondents had been refused formal credit.

Chart 14: Source of start-up capital

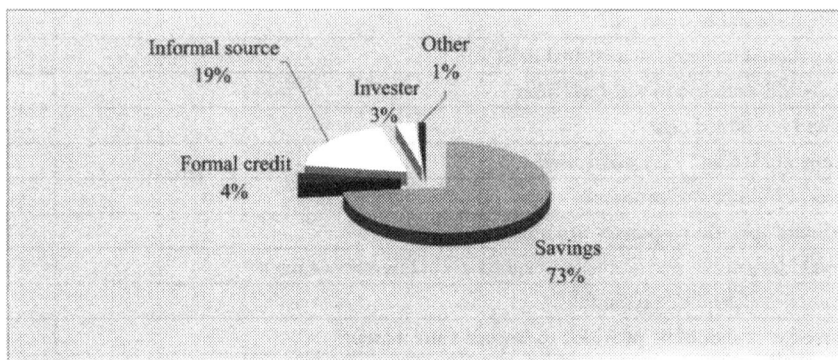

Finance for development: The same pattern continues after start-up. During the last three years of business only 23 per cent had borrowed money while 77 per cent had not. The 34 women who had taken loans were questioned about the source of financing; eight had borrowed from formal sources while 24 had borrowed from informal sources; two had borrowed from both formal and informal sources.

Purpose of borrowing: A multiple response question was asked related to the purpose of borrowing: 68 per cent of borrowers (n = 34) needed money to buy equipment; 44 per cent needed working capital; 18 per cent borrowed for trade finance and 9 per cent for land and buildings. The women who borrowed from formal sources were asked two more questions about collateral and about any problems they faced in obtaining credit. Twenty-seven per cent had used their personal belongings as collateral, 18 per cent pledged their house, 18 per cent used the guarantee of government officers,[54] 9 per cent used dollar account security, and 9 per cent used their immovable property.

Financial information: Women entrepreneurs were asked to give the approximate value of their productive assets, total investment and volume of monthly sales. The following tables provide the responses.

---

[53] Informal source refers to funds from friends and family.
[54] The FWBL was running a small loan scheme in which the guarantees of two government officers could waive the requirement for collateral.

Table 15: Value of productive assets
(Rs. million)
(Excluding land and building)

	Percentage of responses
More than 40	1
From 20 to 40	1
From 0.2 to 20	31
Up to 0.2	61
No response	7

Table 16: Total investment
(Rs. million)

	Percentage of responses
From 10 to 40	2
From 0.5 to 10	1
From 0.2 to 0.5	36
Up to 0.2	61

Table 17: Monthly sales

	Percentage of responses
Rs. 1 million to 5 million	2
Rs. 0.1 million to 1 million	6
Rs. 50,000 to Rs. 0.1 million	6
Rs. 20,001 to Rs. 50,000	39
Up to Rs. 20,000	48

Reinvesting profits: On the subject of reinvesting profits back into the business 39 per cent reinvested more than half their profits in the business; 31 per cent reinvested up to 50 per cent, while 21 per cent reinvested less than a quarter; and 7 per cent said that they did not plough any profits back.

Perceived gender biases in obtaining finance: Respondents were asked whether they thought that being a woman was a major constraint in obtaining formal finance: 66 per cent believed that this was so, while the rest disagreed. The larger group was asked why this should be so: 90 per cent mentioned procedural snags relating to their sex and strict terms of financing.

NON-FINANCIAL SERVICES

Business Support

Non-financial needs: The respondents were specifically asked to indicate four non-financial services that would help their business: 56 per cent indicated marketing; 39 per cent information and business advice; 14 per cent networking with women's organizations; 12 per cent requested subsidized inputs.

Desire for BDS and financial assistance: The respondents were asked to indicate the most important area of their business where they would welcome help from the respective Chamber of Commerce and Industry, related business association and donors. Finance and marketing were at the top, with the following responses.

Table 18: Form of help desired by the women entrepreneurs

Type of help	From Chamber of Commerce	From related business organization	From donors
Finance	39	41	59
Marketing	28	20	26
Training	13	14	7
Networking	10	12	5
Legal	8	11	3

Sources of Business Support: A question was designed to find out if the respondents had received help from any government or private agency in the last three years. Very few (19 per cent) declared that they had received assistance, while the majority (81 per cent) had not received help.

Take-up of business support services: One-quarter of the respondents and 28 per cent of their staff had received some training in the last 3 years while three-quarters had not. The majority of those who received training (92 per cent of women entrepreneurs and 93 per cent of their staff) had undergone skill upgrading.[55] The private sector played a key role in imparting that training. Table 19 shows the percentage share of training by source.

Table 19: Source of training

Source	Women entrepreneurs	Staff
Private institutions	42%	63%
Government institutions	29%	15%
NGO/welfare	10%	15%
Abroad	8%	0%
Others	8%	2%
No response	3%	5%

All the women entrepreneurs said that the training they received was useful, and 83 per cent of employees said the same: 17 per cent thought that it was not useful.

Sources of advice: Respondents were then asked about the person who advised them on business problems. Table 20 provides a sex-disaggregated picture of the answers.

---

[55] Most respondents in the beauty and health business had received training related to new make-up and massage techniques.

Table 20: Advice on business problems[56]

	Percentage of responses			
Family member				71
*Breakdown by sex	Male 81	Female 15	Both 3	No response 1
Relative/friend				17
*Breakdown by sex	Male 2	Female 72	Both 12	No response 8
General manager/Director/Employee				4
Other				12
No response				1

Advice from family and friends: The table above shows that 71 per cent of respondents sought advice from a family member in case of business problems. It is interesting to note that 81 per cent of these referred to their male relatives while only 15 per cent depended on female family members. Only 17 per cent resorted to distant relatives and friends. However, in case of consultation with distant relatives and friends, 72 per cent are likely to be women. (The relations between the enterprise and the family are also explored later at the end of this section.)

Who makes and assists business decisions? Respondents were then asked about the decision-making process in their business. Although the women entrepreneurs ask for business advice from their male family members it seems that they make most of the business decisions by themselves. The incidence is generally high, particularly in recruitment decisions, but relatively low in legal matters.

Table 21: Role of family and others in business decision-making

Decision taker/(s)	Decisions regarding				
	Investments (%)	Recruitment (%)	Marketing/ sales (%)	Public contacts (%)	Signing legal documents (%)
Self	60	72	65	64	59
Husband	8	4	8	4	12
Self/husband	17	9	10	5	8
Relative/friend	7	0	2	9	3
Consultation with management	2	5	5	10	4
Others	6	5	5	7	6
No response	2	5	6	3	7

ASSOCIATIONS

Links to networks and associations: Most women run their enterprise in isolation and do not interact with business associations and networks. Chart 14 shows that 69 per cent had no membership, affiliation or association: 14 per cent were members of Chambers of Commerce and Industry; 17 per cent had registered with the EPB, and 13 per cent belonged to some networking group (with 4 per cent as members of the Pakistan Association of Women Entrepreneurs).[57]

---

[56] The cumulative percentages exceed 100 per cent as some respondents marked more than one factor in the multiple response questions.

[57] There is a strong likelihood of a positive bias towards membership of EPB and the Chamber of Commerce as initially in this survey they were the two major sources of the addresses of women entrepreneurs.

Chart 15: Networking of women entrepreneurs[58]

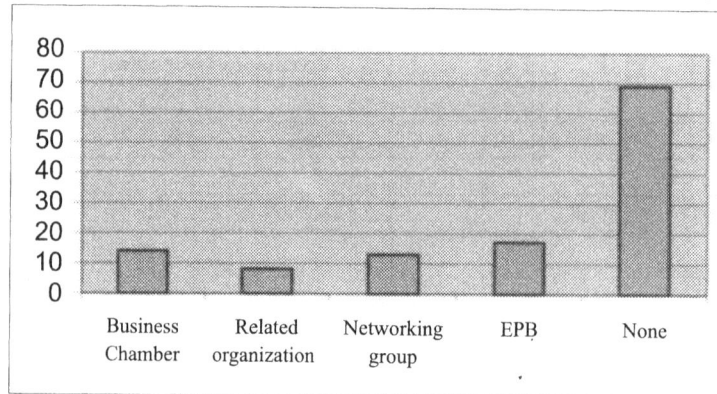

Support from women's organizations: Questions were asked about the respondents' perceptions and expectations of women's support organizations and about their level of outreach. Sixty-six per cent did not know of any such organizations; 7 per cent thought that their range of services was poor; 17 per cent found that their services were not very good, and only 8 per cent said they were good. Thirty-one per cent believed that these organizations needed to improve their outreach; 25 per cent thought they needed to market themselves better, while 15 per cent felt that they should provide business development services. Only 3 per cent of respondents had received assistance from these organizations in the last three years.

Suggestions for women's support organizations: The women entrepreneurs were asked for their recommendations on the role of women's business fora/organizations and their suggestions appear in table 22.

---

[58] The cumulative percentages exceed 100 per cent as some respondents marked more than one factor in the multiple response questions.

Table 22: Expected role of women business fora/organizations[59]

	Percentage of responses
Business development services/solving business issues	**47**
Help women arrange finance	9
Help/solve/advise on business problems/issues	8
Help solve legal problems	7
Suggest solutions to problems at local level	5
Provide business support and facilities for women (exhibitions/seminars)	3
Provide marketing facilities for women (exhibitions)	3
Give training to women	3
Help in solving tax issues	2
Provide assistance in self help	1
Help in making separate market for women	1
Their role is not helpful to us as they don't reach us	4
Lobbying for better business environment	**39**
Special representation of women in administration, policy making to help solve women entrepreneurs' problems	11
Project women entrepreneurs problems through media	7
Create peaceful and safe environment/workplace for women	6
Special treatment for convenience of women	5
Proper representation of small-scale businesswomen in such forums	3
Properly investigate problems by conducting surveys to formulate policies	3
Fight for women's rights	3
Protect from hostile attitude of men	1
Information provision/networking	**26**
Give awareness to women by sharing information	9
Organize themselves/work for betterment/ network for rights	7
Educate women that such helpful organizations exist	4
There should be women clubs at places within easy reach/platforms	3
Play active role by regular meetings/seminars	2
Facilitate women by interactive networking	1
Government-related	**14**
Simplify laws and regulations about business/loans/tax	11
Help women in their interaction with the government	2
Facilitate help from the government	1
Don't know	**8**
No need	**3**
No response	**3**

The information gained from these questions is particularly useful in the context of women entrepreneurs' perceptions of the role, value and potential of various associations, business fora and employers' organizations in supporting women entrepreneurs.

2.2.4. External influences

Major business issues: An open-ended question was used to elicit respondents' views on the major business issues, which — in their opinion — are faced only by women entrepreneurs. This information is valuable as it provides important insights into the range of gender-related issues faced by relatively advantaged women entrepreneurs. The range of responses is listed below.

- Process of getting help from business support organizations is difficult
- Marketing problems
- Household responsibilities
- Getting orders is difficult

---

[59] Multiple response question where percentages may exceed 100 per cent.

- Women are not considered trustworthy and are discouraged from doing business
- Conveyance /transportation problem
- Lack of protection
- Difficulties in management of business
- Dealing with men is difficult/misbehavior
- Image of working women is bad in society/criticism
- Financial matters /loans
- Men create obstacles to women's success
- Women are dishonored in market/not considered respectful
- Late night working hours is a big problem
- Females are ridiculed for being business women
- Male domination in the society and business
- Women don't have decision-making power
- Our business is dependant on others
- To get out in the field/mobility
- Lack of training facilities for women
- Social restrictions
- Problems in legal matters
- Women get deceived by men retailers
- Problems related to business premises
- People's attitude is negative
- Business conditions are not favourable for women in a male dominated society
- Being a women we have to be more formal
- Purdah system (the tradition of veiling)
- To deal with government departments/tax/labour etc. is difficult

Major socio-cultural factors: Respondents were asked to identify the positive and negative social/cultural factors that affect their business activity in Pakistan. Table 23 summarizes their statements.

Table 23: Social/cultural factors affecting women entrepreneurs

Negative	Positive
Male domination	Urban areas are better off because of education
Narrow-mindedness of men/negativism	Teaching is considered respectable in Pakistan
Criticism of women going out	Females are getting more education
Conservative attitude	Girls are learning more skills for business
Bad attitude of people towards working women	Social setup of Pakistan/respect for women
Women are discouraged/dishonored by men	Awareness in women is increasing
Traveling alone is a problem	Labour is cheap
Lack of security	Availability of housemaids at cheap rates
Family restrictions	Popularity of traditional cloth/our culture
Women are not considered trustworthy	Hard working labour
Lack of awareness/illiteracy	Computer education is becoming indispensable
Religious restriction	Embroidery is home based activity
Criticism that daughter's/women's income is a matter of dishonour for the family	Interaction is easy with women in beauty parlour
Can't work freely	Market is expanding for women
Late working hours	Women feel secure with the new transport system
Shop keeping is difficult	Pakistani women are cooperative
To convenience people is difficult	Women from educated family are given respect
People do not understand women's problems	Islamic system of society gives respect to women
No role model for women	People spend much on weddings
Women are deprived of their rights	Good behaviour/attitude of people
Difficult to get recovery from retailers as a woman	Society norms of respect for women
Uncertainty in post marriage life	Educated youth is more respectful
Girl child is oppressed	
Lack of confidence in women	
Attitude of people in marketing is bad	
Dealing with men is not considered worthy	
Dealing with men is considered bad	
Lack of power that men have	
Family responsibilities	
Proper child-care is responsibility of mother	
To take loan is a problem/lack of finance	
Tax problems	
Red tape	
Economic slowdown	
Government officials are troublesome	
Inflation/utility dues	
Government policy is not feasible	
Discrimination	
Elite's monopoly	
Production problems	
Hypocrisy	

Public attitudes to women in business: It is encouraging to note that Pakistani society is increasingly accepting businesswomen. The majority of women entrepreneurs share this perception: 32 per cent believed that the general perception of women in business had improved significantly in the past three years; 36 per cent said that it had improved; 31 per cent did not comment, and only 1 per cent believed that it had worsened. The majority mentioned a positive change of attitudes, new-found trust and confidence in women entrepreneurs, acceptance of women in the business community, greater domestic freedom, and more mobility.

BUSINESS AND THE FAMILY

Balancing business and family: Allocating time for the family and business is a difficult area for most Pakistani women as business engagements normally do not free them from family responsibilities. Chart 16 shows that 11 per cent of respondents devoted 2-5 hours a day to the business while 41 per cent spent that much time with the family. Most of them (65 per cent) devoted 6-9 hours to the business while 41 per cent gave that much time to their family. The highest time commitment of 10 hours or more was given by 24 per cent to business and 17 per cent to the family.

Chart 16: Average number of hours devoted to business and family

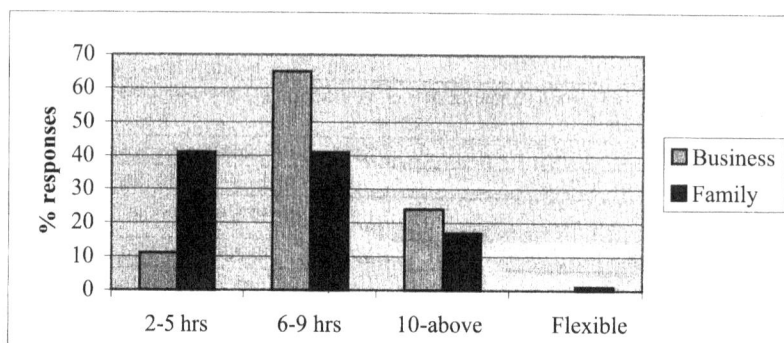

Business and family support: A special section of the questionnaire dealt with family-related matters, and included questions about the level and type of family involvement in the business. Micro and small businesses normally have extensive family connections, and significant family involvement was reported by the respondents. More than 60 per cent had family members helping them to run their business in one way or another;[60] 37 per cent said they were running the business without any family help. Table 24 presents this information broken down by city, size and kind of business. The percentages show that women in manufacturing behave more independently and are less likely to seek family help.

Table 24: Family help in running the business

	All	City		Size of enterprise			Kind of business		
		Lhr.	Isb.	Micro	Small	Medium	Trade	Manufacturing	Service
Base	**150**	**75**	**75**	**78**	**58**	**14**	**29**	**40**	**81**
Nobody	37%	40%	35%	41%	34%	29%	28%	50%	35%
Close blood relations	32%	35%	29%	37%	23%	39%	30%	26%	35%
Relatives by marriage	28%	22%	32%	21%	36%	32%	42%	22%	26%
Other relatives friends	2%	1%	3%	1%	3%	0%	0%	3%	2%
No response	1%	1%	0%	0%	2%	0%	0%	0%	1%

Nature of family involvement: The respondents were further questioned about the patterns of engagement of family members in the business. Table 25 shows that most of the businesses (62 per cent) have one family member in the management team. Further disaggregation of the figures by sex shows that this is much more likely to be a woman (56 per cent) than a man (32 per cent).[61] On the other hand, many businesses (45 per cent) do not have a family member on the supervisory staff, while 42 per cent have one relative. Among supervisory staff the probability is 50 per cent for a woman and 23 per cent for a female relative. The last column shows that the

---

[60] 32 per cent were close blood relations, 28 per cent were relatives by marriage while 2 per cent were distant relatives and friends.
[61] The balance relates to having a person in the management team who is not a family member. In this case the probability of employing a man is 1 per cent, and of employing a woman it is 10 per cent.

40

vast majority of women entrepreneurs (87 per cent), employ more than three family workers in their business.

Table 25: Family members employed in the business

No. of family members	Management staff	Supervisory staff	Workers
0	6%	45%	8%
1	62%	42%	4%
2	19%	10%	1%
3 and above	13%	3%	87%

Contribution to household income: The profits generated by women entrepreneurs make a notable contribution to their total household income. Chart 15 shows that 27 per cent of the respondents contribute more than half of the household income; 31 per cent contribute between a quarter and a half; 29 per cent contribute less than a quarter and 11 per cent contribute nothing.

Chart 17: Women entrepreneurs' contribution to household income

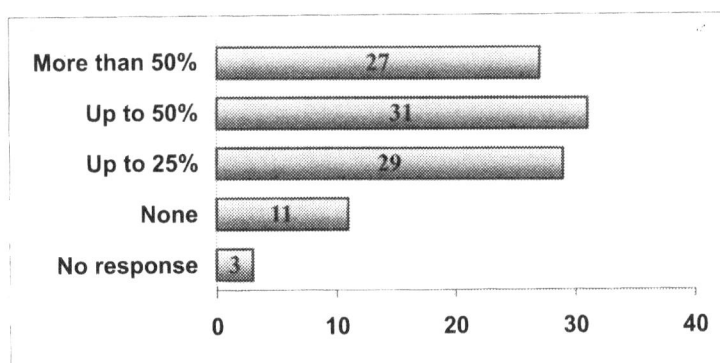

Contribution of others to household income: Another question related to the other family members contributing to the household income. Table 26 provides a comprehensive picture; the first column gives the number of contributing members from 0 to 6 persons, showing that almost every family has more than one income earner. The second column shows that many women entrepreneurs have two or three income earners in the family, most of them men.

41

Table 26: Contribution of family members to household income

Number of family members	% share	Combination of earning family members	Percentage
Nobody	1		
1	41	"1" male and "0" female	90
		"0" male and "1" female	10
2	37	"2" male and "0" female	23
		"1" male and "1" female	73
		"0" male and "2" female	4
3	12	"3" male and "0" female	28
		"2" male and "1" female	50
		"1" male and "2" female	17
		"0" male and "3" female	6
4	4	"3" male and "1" female	50
		"2" male and "2" female	33
		"1" male and "3" female	17
5	3	"3" male and "2" female	75
		"1" male and "4" female	25
6	1	"5" male and "1" female	100
No response	2		

Family attitude to WED: Seventy-one per cent of the surveyed sample were the first women in their family to go into business. Chart 18 shows that families generally reacted positively to the business activity: none of the families reacted badly.[62] We should note, however, that in the prevailing situation in Pakistan it would be extremely difficult for a woman to establish a business in the face of family opposition. Therefore, the views of women who would like to go into business but due to family opposition are unable to do so, will never be heard.

---

[62] This is somewhat unexpected as conventionally elders and men in the family would object to such a decision.

42

Chart 18: Family reaction to their female relative's business activity

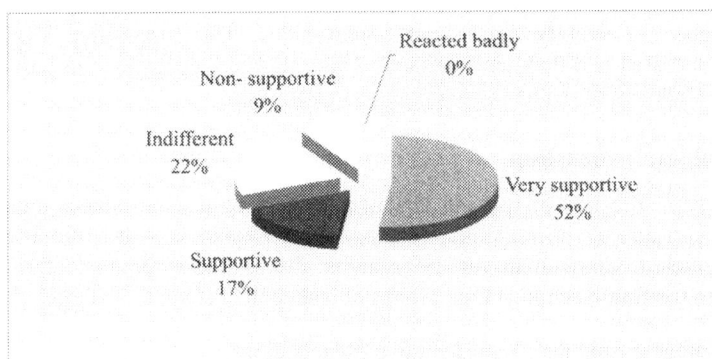

Type of family support: The 104 respondents whose families were either very supportive or supportive were then questioned about the kind of support they received. Further probing by the interviewers yielded the following illustrative responses:

- They helped me in all my difficulties
- They shared my work
- Everybody was supportive and helpful
- Emotional and moral help
- Financial help
- They took care of my children/household work
- They allowed me to do work
- My husband helped me in every way
- My study was professional so they did not have any problem with my doing business
- They asked me to extend this business as they were happy with my business
- Business was time consuming but they accommodated
- They trained me in doing this business
- They allowed me to go out of the house
- They encouraged me by buying my products
- Transportation was provided
- It was a joint project of myself and family members

Thirteen respondents (9 per cent) who faced resistance from their family were questioned further: 69 per cent of them were criticized for not abiding by the traditions; 46 per cent said their families objected to their mobility, while 8 per cent faced personal criticism from within the family.

Impact on family life: The majority of women entrepreneurs thought that doing business had a positive effect on their family life and had improved their image in society (see table 27).

Table 27: Social aspects of doing business

Effect on family life	% response	Social image	% response
Very positive	50	Improved	87
Positive	17	Remained the same	11
Cannot say anything	21	Worsened	1
Negative	11	No response	1
Very negative	1		

3. Recommendations based on the findings from the survey

The recommendations in this section are based upon the findings of the field research which was designed to identify needs and opportunities. The suggestions derive from the outcomes of this research and they are intended to take this project forward in terms of practical action for the development of women entrepreneurs in Pakistan.

3.1 Stakeholders' workshop

This study — the first of its kind in Pakistan — provides some basic understanding of women entrepreneurs and the characteristic features of their businesses. It is proposed that a one-day workshop be held to disseminate this information, discuss the recommendations and involve the stakeholders in the future action. Three groups of stakeholders should be targeted:

- women entrepreneurs and their representative organizations;
- related government institutions;
- multilateral and bilateral donors.

UPDATE: Such a national workshop was organized by the ILO in Lahore on 15 February 2002, and considerable interest was shown by the Government agencies, donors and development partners in the preliminary findings of the survey report. (A summary of the workshop recommendations is provided as an appendix to this report.)

3.2 Preparation of a comprehensive database of women entrepreneurs

Practically no hard data are available on women entrepreneurs in Pakistan. Government departments and the business associations/networking organizations have no information on the total number of women entrepreneurs, their lines of business, value added, employment or related information. Various attempts have been made by organizations such as EPB and FWBL to develop data sets, but the results are far from satisfactory and the information is not regularly updated. It is therefore recommended that a comprehensive database of women entrepreneurs in Pakistan should be prepared and used in future research and action plans.

3.3 Gender audit of SME development institutions

There is a small number of federal and provincial institutions working specifically for the development of SMEs. The survey results show that they do not reach out to women entrepreneurs; their operations are normally targeted at businessmen as business is generally considered a male domain in Pakistan. It is proposed that one such institution should be selected for a gender audit of its operations. SMEDA, a federal institution dedicated to providing enterprise development services, might be a suitable candidate. The gender audit would identify gaps and distortions in existing services that could be rectified in future operations.

3.4 Entrepreneurship development programmes for potential women entrepreneurs

The survey results show that the probability of doing business increases significantly for Pakistani women if they have acquired a formal education. Other findings reveal that the rate of business start-up among women has increased considerably in the last decade. A majority of the surveyed sample consisted of women entrepreneurs who were housewives, employed or students before starting their businesses. This suggests that an opportunity exists to tap the potential of would-be women entrepreneurs in these three groups. A comprehensive module on entrepreneurship could be developed and introduced in the Master's courses at the First Women's University, Rawalpindi as a pilot project. This course could subsequently be extended to other institutions and even run by SME development institutions.

UPDATE: At least two new postgraduate courses have been launched on the theme of entrepreneurship, with an emphasis on women.

3.5 Hand-holding and counselling of selected women entrepreneurs to generate role models

Finance and marketing emerge as the two major demands of women entrepreneurs. It is recommended that a pilot project be launched for a selected group of 25 to 50 businesswomen in each of the four provinces of Pakistan to prepare a new group of successful women entrepreneurs to serve as role models. A multilateral arrangement is proposed including ILO as facilitating consultant, a donor agency or development bank such as the Asian Development Bank for funding, and Pakistani government institutions as executing agencies. The criteria for selecting the women entrepreneurs could be agreed through mutual consultations. The proposed government institutions would be FWBL (finance), SMEDA (supply-side issues) and EPB (international marketing).

3.6 Establishing/strengthening women's business fora

The small number of women's business fora existing in Pakistan have extremely limited outreach and offer few quality services. They do not exist as institutions but as personalities: they have limited membership and confined regional outreach. This explains why no such business forum has emerged as a national lobby group for women entrepreneurs. There is an urgent need to assist the existing fora to organize as self-sustaining institutions, to revitalize those associated with the regional Chambers of Commerce, the Employers' Federation of Pakistan, or to establish a new institution which could represent women entrepreneurs at national level.

UPDATE: In order to move forward with these and other proposals, in particular those ideas emerging from ILO's national workshop on women's entrepreneurship development held in Lahore in February 2002, the ILO has prepared a summary project proposal to address some of the most pressing issues. (See appendix for details of this proposal.)

PART III

4. Profiles of twenty women entrepreneurs in MSEs in Pakistan

The last part of this report comprises of stories of 20 women entrepreneurs. These women entrepreneurs were selected from the survey sample. They come from different backgrounds and are engaged in a variety of businesses. Each one of them has a unique story of starting and doing business.

4.1 Ambreen Bukhari
Menika Mines, Islamabad

Ambreen faced a volley of troubles and criticism when she dared to enter into a difficult business. She collects, cuts and exports precious stones and prepares studded jewelry for the domestic market. Nobody believed her when she decided to do this business 11 years back. It was considered a purely male domain, as one is supposed to travel to the mountains, interact with male entrepreneurs for the management of backward and forward linkages of the business, and to explore actively for the niche markets. Many of her colleagues thought that it would be insulting for men that a female entrepreneur wanted to do this business, but she started it and is successful at it. She completed her post-graduate studies abroad and specialized in geology. She divorced and returned to Pakistan with her two daughters and started this business soon after in what for her were very difficult circumstances. However, she was confident and wanted to make herself stronger so as to support her children and to be able to tackle the cruelties in life. That made her fearless in her resolve to do business and to fight against all odds. Today she has full floor showroom for her jewelry in a business center in the most famous market of Islamabad. She also arranges exhibitions in Islamabad and Karachi and has participated in international events. She is a leading exporter of precious stones and has represented Pakistan at a couple of international forums. She also works as a consultant and imparts training in stone-cutting techniques.

4.2 Ayesha Zeenat
Pappasalis, Islamabad

Ayesha Zeenat, better known as Gina, has given a practical shape and form to her academic specialization. She did a Diploma in Hotel and Restaurant Management from the Conrad Hilton College, University of Houston. After working as an intern for various restaurants as chef-helper, accounts assistant and various other restaurant-related jobs, she had the strong realization that there was no future in seeking a good job in this field. She then decided to do something on her own and started the first original Italian restaurant in Islamabad. Her father provided financing for the project. It was as a big risk, as Islamabad was not an easy city for a food business. However, what started as an eight-table restaurant, proved a success from day one. It was the right concept at the right time. Islamabad had no international food chain and an Italian restaurant proved a treat for customers. Under the able supervision of Gina, and her original recipes, the small eatery, which started in 1989, has flourished into a double storey, 40-table restaurant in Islamabad, with another branch in Karachi. Since 1998, Gina has expanded her food business by adding a café for light snacks, Bistro Alfredo. However, a name-sake restaurant opened in Lahore last year. Gina had to fight a legal case to save her franchise and won the case successfully. Pure dedication and hard work have enabled Gina to maintain an ever-rising progress in the food business. Gina expresses the secret of her success by saying "I have always kept a strong check on the working conditions at my restaurant, and try to maintain a personal rapport with all my customers"

4.3 Firdous Huda
Firdousi Beauty Parlour, Islamabad

Firdous is of the view that the business environment for women entrepreneurs is getting better gradually. She has three children and started her own beauty parlour 12 years before. She started working in the famous beauty parlour Depilex first. Having served there for years, she went abroad and got married. She has three children and eventually separated from her husband.

She completed a couple of beautician courses abroad and then returned to Pakistan. Her father encouraged her to start a business and provided financing as well. Her brother did not appreciate the idea though. However, she was constrained to do something to take care of herself and her three children. She started her business in the ground floor of her house, and moved upstairs to live on the first floor with her children. The business soon became popular and she felt that she needed to arrange a separate place for it. She did not have resources to do so. She kept working hard to save money until she could get her present premises. Firdous believes in a personalized service for her customers. She says that the quality and standard of her service together are enough to market her business, and she does not need any more marketing effort than that. She has 16 female employees and plans to expand her business to other cities. She understands that for women doing business is difficult as they have to bear children and raise them, while male entrepreneurs absolve themselves from these responsibilities. She is confident though, that everything is possible in life through sheer hard work and dedication.

4.4 Naheed Fatima
Tution Centre, Rawalpindi

Naheed started her tuition center five years ago. She wanted to open a school but was scared of the lengthy process, finding the start-up capital, and the taxes of the government. "I come from a lower-middle class so I did not have much resources to start a school. I did not have collateral so there were no chances of getting formal financing. I did not have connections in the government to manage the registration and taxation processes, so I decided to go for a tuition center; a more informal option", she recollects. She had never entered into a business before and was a bit reluctant to take any risks, so she decided to make a very humble start. The major reason behind starting this center was the economic difficulties that her family was facing. She had graduated some years before, as did her sisters, but they were all dependent upon the meager income generated by their male members of the family. The small income of the family and rising inflation persuaded Naheed's family to support her in running this center. The family was very helpful as they thought that this business did not involve any male interaction, as she exclusively focused on female students. Soon two of her sisters joined her as they were unemployed and they recruited two more teachers to start instruction in other subjects as well. Naheed is now running a successful tuition center and intends to expand it further as a model school. She has gained a lot of business confidence, but is not very sure how long it is going to take to start a fully-fledged school. She is a bit unhappy about the plight of women in Pakistan, and is wary of the fact that females are in a very weak bargaining position in society. As a woman she feels very insecure in the Pakistani society.

4.5 Parveen Shahid
Roop Boutique, Islamabad

Parveen did her Masters in Psychology from Karachi University and never underwent any formal training related to her present business. She started teaching in a local college where she used to participate actively in extra-curricular activities like Students' Week. The week used to have design competitions, and she won prizes many times for designing the best clothes at the least expensive prices. This is how she discovered an artist within herself, which gave her confidence to start designing clothes and develop the skills that she had learnt from her mother as a child. Most of the people appreciated her designs and she decided to enter into the business she is in now. Two big reasons were the availability of seed money and the help extended by her husband. She faced a number of problems in the beginning. But the problems with the male workers were very pronounced — their attitudes were irresponsible and defiant and sometimes hostile. But gradually she became experienced in dealing with them. Today she is running a business in Islamabad and deals in formal, informal and bridal wear. She employs 13 workers and 12 of them are males. She still feels that there is a communication and understanding gap between her and the workers, but she cannot help it. Parveen says that her business has made her very busy and most of her relatives complain that she does not socialize with them. She is of the opinion that male interaction is a major constraint for the women doing business in Pakistan, as the society has a tunnel vision and very conservative attitudes towards women.

4.6   Shagufta Rana
Saint Jacob Cambridge School, Islamabad

Shagufta is the first women in her family who has ever established a business. She is married with no children and believes that getting and spreading education is the duty of each member of the Muslim community. She decided to start this school partly because she had done her undergraduate studies in Education, and partly because there was no English medium school in the vicinity. She rented a building which, for her, was a difficult task, and she started the school in 1996. "I did not have any business experience, but my family was excited about this new development and my father, mother and sisters helped me a lot to get this business going", she exclaims. The early years were really tough, as the number of students was much less than what she required to break even. She had spent her savings on renting the building and purchasing necessary furniture and equipment. No financial institution was ready to lend without collateral, and the expenses were overshooting the income. In the meantime she got married and her husband helped her to overcome the business difficulties and reorient the business. The school is well on its way now, and offers courses from class 1 to 10 and employs 13 female teachers. Shagufta intends to expand the scale and scope of her business now. She wants to turn this school into a college where she could start the classes of FA/F.Sc as well. She thinks that imparting education to others is a huge responsibility, and that the government should provide more facilities to the people associated with this noble service.

4.7   Shahida Syed
New Baby Garments, Rawalpindi

Shahida is a self-made entrepreneur who started her business at a very micro level in 1989. She had not had a lot of education, and her family was living hand-to-mouth when she decided to start stitching clothes at home. Most of her customers liked her stitching and she spread the word in the vicinity that she could provide this service at cheap rates and with good quality. The tiny business grew very slowly in the beginning, but three years on she had to include her sister in the business. Her brother was the next to follow to take care of marketing. She did not have any prior business experience and was unaware of the cost of inputs, but she learnt everything by doing it herself. Most of her relatives and acquaintances discouraged her as they thought that it was a "curse" for a woman to step out of her house to indulge in business, but she did it because she had to do it for sheer survival reasons. When the business expanded she decided to seek a loan. She was fortunate to get Rs. 25,000 from the First Women Bank on the personal guarantee of two government officers. After gaining more business confidence she started selling clothes to the shopkeepers in the market on credit. However, most of the male retailers were callous and exploited her weak bargaining position by delaying or denying payments. Then she added her brother to her marketing team and selected only those retailers who were more reliable. She added some more women workers in her production team when demand increased. The next step was to specialize in children's garments, and later in embroidered ladies garments. Today she is running this business successfully and has a team of 15 employees including two males. She operates in the local market and intends to hire a manager and start exporting her products, but has no idea about engaging in export business.

4.8   Dr. Shakila
Shafi Hospital, Rawalpindi

"The biggest problem for women in business is men, as they dominate every kind of activity in Pakistan", says Shakila. She also lauds her husband who has been very supportive of her in establishing and doing her medical services business. She used to have a government job at the Pakistan Institute of Medical Sciences (PIMS) in Islamabad, but it started to become increasingly difficult for her as she had to commute a long distance. She also wanted to spend more time with her children, which was not possible after everyday's work commitments. Then she decided to open her own small hospital near her home. She bought a piece of land with the help of her husband and established her medical clinic. There was no lady doctor in that area at that time, but even still very few patients turned up in the beginning. The area where she is running a clinic is predominantly backward and most of the residents are illiterate. She bought an x-ray machine and ultrasound equipment for the use of her patients. "It is a slow process to win the confidence of people and make them use modern facilities as they are conditioned to using traditional methods", she laments. But she is continuing with her profession, as she believes that she is not simply running a business, but doing a noble job. She is very grateful to her husband for his great support, without which her business would not have been possible. She employs 13 people and takes most of business decisions with the help of her husband.

4.9 Talat Peerzada
Muitat, Islamabad

Talat has three children. She had been very fond of Chinese cuisine right from her childhood. She used to cook it herself, and always kept herself busy with new cuisine and doing experiments for improving their taste. Her family and friends always appreciated her cooking abilities, but she had never thought of marketing her ideas until her husband, who works for Pakistan Army, was posted to a far-off place. She had to stay in Islamabad for her children's schooling. That was the crucial time when she decided to establish a Chinese restaurant to kill her boredom, and to use her time in a productive way. She thought that it would be a good experience for her, and she would be able to earn some money that could be used to educate her children better. Right from the beginning she was very confident that her business would thrive, although she soon felt that the general public did not appreciate having a lady sitting at the reception desk of a restaurant and managing five male employees. She faced some initial hiccups in her business, but it progressed more or less smoothly right from the beginning. "It was quite difficult to mange everything, from buying fresh vegetables to preparing large quantity of food with the same taste and freshness", she recalls. She had to put in long hours at the restaurant and take care of the quality of food and service, but it has paid her back well. Today she is running a successful restaurant which is popular for its quality of food and service. She started a home delivery service more than a year ago and this is going very well. Talat is of the opinion that women entrepreneurs need help in dealing with the government, and especially the income tax officials.

4.10 Uzma Gul
Varan Tours, Sadar , Rawalpindi

Uzma Gul established a transport company initially with only one bus, and now the company owns a fleet of 75 buses, which are running on various routes of Rawalpindi and Islamabad. Transport is considered to be a very difficult domain where even the male entrepreneurs fear to enter — but Uzma dared to. She wanted to dispel the notion that woman entrepreneurs restrict themselves to certain traditional businesses. Uzma has been associated with this business for the last 10 years, and is looking forward to expanding her business. She faced a multitude of problems in the beginning. One big problem was inconsistency in the transport policies of successive governments. "The only thing that remained consistent was a negative attitude of the government officials. They felt very awkward to deal with a woman transporter", she recollects. Within the company she faced administrative problems and a strange form of resentment from the staff, as they were very uneasy to have a woman boss. Uzma started with an inter-city service between Sargodha and Rawalpindi, and later expanded to the twin cities of Islamabad and Rawalpindi. Along with the profit motive, she wanted to start a quality transport service for the working women, which was hitherto absent. Uzma believes that one can only achieve things through hard work, commitment, courage and a little bit of craziness. "I have also learnt that it is a male-oriented society out there, and a woman cannot perform well if the male members of her family do not create a right kind of environment for her. Your family should be very supportive, otherwise you cannot do anything in this society, and I have been quite lucky in this regard", she concludes.

4.11 Adeeba Talat
Lok Virsa Boutique, Lahore

Adeeba got married at the age of 15. She had hardly finished her matriculation at that time. She is 40 now, the mother of five children, and running her own business for the last 10 years. Adeeba was very fond of dress designing from the beginning, and her mother-in-law encouraged her to start designing and selling clothes. She was short of money and wanted to be independent as well. Hence she decided to do her own business, and she chose crochet lace clothes to start with. The idea caught on quickly as it was relatively new in the market and public response was very good. This gave her some business confidence and she decided to expand by making outfits to be sold in the market. She made a verbal contract with a local shopkeeper to sell her clothes by displaying at his shop. This turned out to be a very bad experience. The treacherous shopkeeper sold her clothes but never paid her. She was not the only one who became the victim of a male retailer. Many of her friends told her that their small initiatives had met with the same fate. Disgruntled and disappointed, Adeeba decided not to use this marketing channel any more but resolved to carry on with her business. She changed her strategy and started direct marketing by participating in the local exhibitions and fun-fairs. A moderate response in the beginning soon turned into a good stream of orders. These days she serves a number of clients, but produces only to order. Her husband manages the marketing and sales, while she manages designing and production. Adeeba intends to expand her business and enter into the export market. The main purpose behind earning more money is to send her son abroad for higher education. She has recently sent some designs to her sister who lives in the USA and is expecting to get some orders from there.

4.12 Anjum Rafi
Qashang Boutique and Heritage School System, Lahore

Anjum is of the view that although Pakistan is a male-dominated society, now men have started accepting that women are able to do many things other than household work. Having completed a Master's degree in Textiles, she decided to start "Heritage School System" about 13 years ago. It had established a good reputation within a couple of years. She was not very satisfied though, as operating a school had not been a passion in her life. She always had a creative bent, and she used to design dresses when she was a schoolgirl. This is why she decided to take up the field of textiles for her specialization, where she could tap her creativity and do something that was more fulfilling and close to her aptitude. Having established a school of repute, she decided to diversify her business in 1993 and started a boutique. It was a very small one in the beginning but started growing swiftly. Today she specializes in bridal and formal wear for women and will soon be exporting to a couple of foreign markets. She thinks that the crucial factor in her success has been her knowledge of the sector and her designing sense. To her understanding, this is a must for every businessperson in the garments' sector as it is very competitive. In the beginning she had difficulties in finding skilled labour and different fabric materials for dresses in the beginning, but she managed it with the help of her husband to whom she is very thankful for all kinds of support. Anjum is a member of Lahore Chamber of Commerce and Industry, Pakistan Association of Women Entrepreneurs, and the Export Promotion Bureau. She is very optimistic about her business, and is planning to participate in exhibitions and fashion shows abroad.

4.13 Asma Mehmood
Multani Dresses, Lahore

After having three daughters and when the youngest was aged 6, Asma decided to enter into a business to earn money and spend her free time usefully. Today she employs 35 women and 20 men who work to produce traditional dresses and embroidery that are sold in Lahore. She hails from Southern Punjab, the least-developed area of the province of Punjab where literacy and other social indicators are very poor. Coming from an area that has stringent social and cultural traditions, and where mobility of women is very limited, she dared to start her own business. Luckily enough, she had the support of her husband and family that helped to mitigate these social and cultural problems. Inexperienced in business and barely literate, Asma was fearful of travelling alone in the beginning. In her own words, "Travelling alone is not safe for women, and you cannot get a secure place to stay overnight in other cities" she stated, but her business involved a lot of travel. Gradually she became confident, and her undaunting resolve to make this business a success helped her to keep on track. Asma is disgruntled about the government's policies in general, and tax policies in particular. She is of the opinion that unfavourable regulations and tax policies have negatively affected her business. She could have fared much better if she could have obtained a loan from a financial institution for her business. She tried to obtain a loan once, but gave up after some time having encountered countless procedural snags and the hostile attitude of bankers towards her small business. Daily she spends almost 7 hours on average in her business. She believes in hard work, and takes all the business decisions by herself and believes that she could do wonders if her husband were also to join her in the business.

4.14   Bushra Iqbal
Bushra Iqbal Beauty Clinic, Lahore

Bushra was very business-oriented right from her childhood. She established a library of 100 children-books when she was merely 9 and used to lend out those books. "This is how I started my first venture", she recollects. She got married at the age of 18, and soon after went to Germany for cosmetic treatment to get rid of freckles and pimples. There she got to know about the modern make-up techniques, and other means and techniques to keep her looking fresh. She was inspired by this experience and thought of learning those techniques to start a business of her own. This led her to join Hannereuh beauty clinic for a diploma course. It was an interesting experience and she ended up specializing in Hairdo, Bridal make-up, Medicare and Pedicure, Massage and Facial techniques. Having finished those courses in more than two years, she started working in the same institute. She returned to Lahore in 1966 and started her own beauty clinic at a time when the profession of a beautician was rather new in Pakistan. She has spent 35 years in this business by now. As a pioneer though, she had to face a number of problems. "The worst of all was dealing with the orthodox government officials", she recalls. She did not have her own premises to start this business, so she rented one. She had no money for machinery and equipment, so she borrowed some from her brother and worked very hard with that tiny amount to make her business a success. The business was very demanding, and so were her family commitments. The good thing was the relentless support of her family, and especially of her husband, which kept her progressing. These days she is busy turning her beauty parlour into a beauty clinic, and she is sure that her expertise and sheer hard work would soon turn it into one of the best in the town.

4.15   Farah Yousuf
Comeily Collection, Lahore

"Doing business is the responsibility of men. Why are women doing it?" This is how Farah thinks Pakistani society responds to women doing business. Farah Yousuf was only 18 when she got married to a chartered accountant in Karachi. She came to Lahore after her marriage and completed her bachelor's degree. Her father encouraged her to start a small business in the garments sector, as it was her hobby to design clothes for the family. She took his advice and started operating at a very small level by holding exhibitions at the Hotel Pearl Continental with the collaboration of different designers, and using her own brand name. Soon the brand name became popular and she started selling at all the shopping malls at Lahore. She then expanded her business to Karachi, which was again a success. She joined Lahore Chamber of Commerce and Industry in 1998 and became a member of the Women Entrepreneur Society of Pakistan. She visited Australia, Jeddah and India with trade delegations to enter into the export market. However, her business was facing a financial crunch at that time. She had spent all her savings, but she desperately needed working capital. She contacted a couple of financial institutions but could not manage to get financing. In the meantime, one of her partners ditched her and the whole business plunged into troubles. That was a great setback to the business and it took her some time to recover from this. Her husband and family helped her to come out of this and she rejuvenated her business in February 2001. These days she is in the process of tapping some international customers, and she is showing new hope and vigor.

4.16 Nasreen Akhtar
New Lampshades, Lahore

"Doing a business for women in Pakistan is like walking on a tight-rope as one has to balance between family and business. This is really tough, as business responsibilities do not exonerate women from the family responsibilities". Nasreen Akhtar comes from a typical business family and her husband is also a businessman. She completed her matriculation, and got married at the age of 30. She had a good flair for business right from the beginning, and had been working as an associate with her husband since getting married 12 years earlier. The right time to establish her independent business came when her third daughter started going to school and she got some free time to concentrate on activities other than the household chores. She accompanied her husband and traveled to England to do a market survey and get some ideas for export business. She got her first order for lampshades with the help of her husband. She was very excited to have an independent assignment and completed that consignment with great success. This gave her confidence in continuing this business and making a relationship of the trust she had established with her customer. The customer invited her to establish a joint venture in Pakistan for making lampshades. He also provided free machinery and technology to establish a manufacturing unit in Pakistan. She put her heart and soul in this project, but unfortunately the next two years were full of difficulties and problems for her. The interaction with different government departments for getting clearance and licenses was so cumbersome that she could only get that machinery cleared after a long struggle of two years. Getting the machinery and having it installed was not the end of the story, as the government officials kept on creating problems. "Those two years taught me a lot and it was a very stressful period", she recalls. But finally she managed to get out of that difficult period. She is very thankful to her husband who has been instrumental in getting orders, marketing her products and helping her solving these problems. The majority of her existing workers are females. She intends to expand her business and vows to employ more female workers in the near future.

4.17 Robina Jamil
Lahore

Robina left her job 10 years ago when her family underwent severe financial distress. She then started a business of assembling toys, plastic clips and imitation jewelry with the help of her father and brother. "It was quite tough in the beginning", she recalls. My family was very supportive as we were under financial distress and I was one of the earning family members, but the attitude of distant family and friends was derogatory as they looked down upon me for my unworthy interaction with the male customers. Robina had a very humble start. First she had some informal training on joining the different parts of toys together and established a small business. The crucial step was to get her first order, which proved to be a really difficult task. She hired two women and trained them to market her products, but it turned out to be a futile effort. The major hurdle in getting orders was her employees were women, as both the wholesalers and retailers were reluctant to do business with women dealers. Most of the time they inquired about the owner of the business and were further disappointed to know that she was a lady as well. "Most of the traders did not trust me as I was a woman", Robina recollects, "so I had to ask my brother and father to help me in getting orders". They also had to get involved in the supply of products, as mobility for my women employees was a problem and the male traders were not very courteous. The business has graduated from its infancy stage. I have built a network now on the basis of the trust that we have developed over the last ten years. Things are a little better now, partly because I have become a bit experienced in the business, and partly because I am used to the problems that one has to face as a woman entrepreneur in Pakistan.

4.18 Sobia Qadir Khan
Sobia Khan's, Lahore

As a young businesswoman Sobia is skeptical about the continuation of her business. The biggest threat she faces is the uncertainty of business after her marriage. " I cannot develop my business to the extent I want to, because I don't know the situation after my marriage. I don't know if I am going to stay in Pakistan or go abroad!" Sobia feels strongly that there is a positive change in the societal attitude towards the women doing business, but the perceptions based on the stereotyped roles of women in a patriarchal society like Pakistan are a big constraint. She thinks that a change is taking place, and society in general has started recognizing that females are more brilliant than their male counterparts. This may eventually demystify the outmoded stereotypes in the future, but the change is slow. Sobia did her B.Sc. in Home Economics in 1997, and did some professional courses in fabric and block printing, and a diploma in fashion design. Right after the diploma, she participated in her first exhibition along with two partners. It turned out to be a stunning success. The partners somehow pulled out, but she forged ahead with high hopes and great ambitions. Her mother played a major role in terms of financial and emotional support to start and sustain the business. The most depressing part of the start-up was the attitude of labour. She was annoyed as the labourers took a female boss for granted as she did not assert much in the beginning, but gradually she learnt to deal with them. Now the business is running smoothly, and she plans to expand her operations in the international market. She has plans to open a stitching school for females, as she is a staunch believer in women earning their own living. The ambitions stay in her head, nevertheless with great apprehension about the future of her business after her marriage.

4.19   Zeenat Saboohi
Jianney Trades, Lahore

Zeenat ventured to establish a sports manufacturing unit almost seven years ago, and dared to enter into a field that is generally considered a male domain. She started this business with three objectives: to help the poor people by giving them employment; to produce quality products for exports to help the country meet its foreign exchange requirements, and to make money for herself and her family. In a short period of seven years she has emerged as a producer of footballs, baseballs and basketballs which are being exported to a number of countries. She started this business by herself and her family was very supportive to her in setting up this business. She participates in international trade fairs, which are a good source of getting orders for her products. She has undergone training recently and intends to get ISO 9002 certification for her business as early as possible. She has not faced any specific gender-related problems in marketing her products. Her only concern is that the costs of her inputs have gone so high, which is eroding the competitive edge of her products in the international market. Most of her products are sold in the international market and the Export Promotion Bureau of the Government of Pakistan has played an instrumental role in introducing her to these export markets. She looks forward to obtaining some more government support in terms of short-term capital financing. She works for 12 hours a day at an average. Having 4 children, she can spare only 2 to 3 hours in a day for her family. In her opinion Pakistani society is slowly getting more mature and responsible, and she feels that doing business has raised her status in society.

4.20   Zoya Aleem
Herbal Workshop, Lahore

Zoya was deeply inspired by her grandmother who was a doctor of traditional Greek medicine. She developed an interest in herbs that her grandmother used to use for medicines. Although she did her Masters degree in Journalism, her passion had always been in working with herbs and their effective use for the benefit of humankind. This led her to start "The Herbal Workshop" 10 years ago. She was very lucky to have a supporter like her husband. She comes from a traditional Pakistani family, but her husband stood all the way with her to help her to establish and run this business. "He supports me from the core of his heart", Zoya says. In answering the question about the difficulties that she had to face while starting this business, she regrets the limited role that government support offers to businesswomen. She complained that the procedure of getting loans from the financial institutions is cumbersome — it is rather impossible. She is of the opinion that it is a waste of one's time even to think of getting government financing for one's business. "Dealing with the government is awful", she maintains. It is difficult to get registered as a taxpayer, and even difficult to deal with the government officials thereafter. Her business is going well, and she wants to have her own production units in place very soon. She has been promoting her products through different channels, and is doing a television programme on beauty care as well.

References

Ahmed Karim, N. (2001), "Jobs, Gender and Small Enterprises in Bangladesh: Factors Affecting Women Entrepreneurs in Small and Cottage Industries in Bangladesh", Geneva, ILO, SEED/WEDGE Working Paper No. 14.

Akmal Hussain Dr. 1994 "Poverty Alleviation in Pakistan" Vanguard Books Lahore Pakistan.

Bezhani, M. (2001), "Women Entrepreneurs in Albania", Geneva, ILO, SEED/WEDGE Working Paper No. 21.

Ferdinand, C. (2001), "Jobs, Gender and Small Enterprises in the Caribbean: Lessons from Barbados, Suriname and Trinidad and Tobago", Geneva, ILO, SEED/WEDGE Working Paper No. 19.

FWBL; First in Concept, second to none (Pamphlet of FWBL).

First Women Bank Limited; Annual Report 2000.

"Globalization and the Apparel Industry of Pakistan" presented by SMEDA at the ILO sub regional conference on Competitiveness, Productivity and job Quality in the Garments Industry in South Asia, 25-26 September 2001.

Human Development Report 1999, UNDP, New York.

Human Development Report 2000, UNDP, New York.

"Identification of Women's Small Entrepreneurship Development Support Project in the Province of the Punjab" submitted to the Royal Netherlands Embassy, Islamabad by shirkat Gah and Entrepreneurial Development and Advisory Services (EDAS), Lahore (no date mentioned).

Kantor, P. (2001), "Promoting Women's Entrepreneurship Development based on Good Practice Programmes: Some Experiences from the North to the South", Geneva, ILO, SEED/WEDGE Working Paper No. 9.

Khan N. S., and Shaheed, F. (1984), "Women's Skill Development and Income Generating Schemes and Projects in the Punjab" report prepared for the UNICEF.

Mayoux, L. (2001), "Jobs, Gender and Small Enterprises: Getting the Policy Environment Right", Geneva, ILO, SEED/WEDGE Working Paper No. 15.

Naseem. S. M., "Government and NGO Programmes in the Alleviation of Poverty in Pakistan" draft report submitted to the World Bank, Pakistan March 2001.

"National IT Survey" Top line Results conducted by Gallup Pakistan for IT and Telecommunication Division, Ministry of Science of Technology, Islamabad.

National Population and Housing Census of Pakistan 1998 published 2000, Statistics Division, Government of Pakistan, Islamabad.

Nichols Marcucci, P. (2001), "Jobs, Gender and Small Enterprises in Africa and Asia: Lessons drawn from Bangladesh, the Philippines, Tunisia and Zimbabwe, Geneva, ILO, SEED/WEDGE Working Paper No. 18.

Pakistan Statistical Yearbook 2001, Federal Bureau of Statistics Division, Government of Pakistan, Islamabad.

Preparatory Assistance (PA) Document Number: PAK/96/016 — "Facilitating Women's Mobility" UNDP Pakistan.

Samina Kamal 1997, Women Empowerment and Poverty Alleviation in South Asia: "The Dual benefits of Microcredit" p. 114 South Asia Poverty Alleviation Program UNDP.

Shahnaz Kazi "Gender Inequalities and Development in Pakistan" in the *50 Years of Pakistan's Economy* ed. Rafi Khan, Shahrukh, Oxford University Press 2000, Islamabad.

Stiglitz Joseph 1998 "Gender and Development: The Role of the State" Gender and Development workshop, Washington, D.C.

Stoyanovska, A. (2001), "Jobs, Gender and Small Enterprises in Bulgaria", Geneva, ILO, SEED/WEDGE Working Paper No. 20.

Study of FWBL and Recommended JICA Assistance to FWBL: A study by JICA, Pakistan 1997.

Ten Year Development Perspective Plan (2001-11) and Three Year Development Programme (2001-4), Government of Pakistan, Planning Commission Islamabad, September 1, 2001.

World Bank Report of "Country Gender Profile of Pakistan" (http://www.worldbank.org/gender/info/pakist.htm)

Women and the Pakistan Government: A Brief Policy History (1975-1998) UNDP, Islamabad.

"Women Entrepreneurs in Pakistan" A Directory of Manufacturers and Exporters 1998/99, Export promotion Bureau, Karachi Government of Pakistan.

Appendix A

Gender and Development: Ten-Year Perspective Development Plan, 2001-11

Planning Commission of Pakistan, Islamabad

ISSUES	STRATEGIES	PROGRAMMES
• Institutional Mechanism for the advancement of Women through Employment.	• Development of a national policy for women. • Preparation of a Strategic Plan for Women Development. • Setting up of a Management Information System. • Creation of Technical Resource Base in the Women Study Centers. • Gender Sensitization at Federal, Provincial & District level. • Capacity Building of Women councilors.	• Policy formulation process in consultation with stake-holders. • Mainstreaming of Gender and Development through sectoral programme. • Establish a data base for gender statistics. • Upgrade Women Study centers in Resource Centers. • Orientation courses/workshops for elected women representatives. • Gender sensitization training.
• Women & Poverty	• Implementation of National Plan of Action. • Economic Empowerment of Women.	• Gender & Poverty Alleviation & skill development projects. • Micro financing through different windows. • Monitoring & Evaluation.
• Human Rights, legal issues and violence against women.	• Family protection programme. • National Commission on the status of women. • Advocacy and awareness.	• Development of family protection complexes, to include crisis centers, Darual-Aman and shelters linked with legal aid, police centers, family courts and others. • Awareness through Mass Media.

Appendix B:

Report on National Policy of Development and Empowerment of Women

13 December 2002 (c/o Pakistan Press International Information Services)

The Government under General Pervez Musharraf, President of Pakistan has taken many steps which are landmarks for the women of Pakistan. Amongst them, is the formulation of the first ever National Policy for Development and Empowerment of Women.

In support of Government's policy of public-private partnership, it is stated with pleasure that the ownership of this policy rests with the stakeholders. It is the outcome of an exhaustive countrywide consultative process which stretched over a year and extended from grass-root to national level, using all the information media available, thus obtaining the broadest national consensus to support its content.

It contains a Vision, Goal, Aims and Objectives, lays down the guiding principles, gives the key policy measures, specifically addressing the empowerment dimensions in the social, economic and political fields. The crosscutting issues are fully reflected in identification of the key policy measures. These measures have been drawn from the National Health Policy, Education Sector Reforms, Labour Policy, Access to Justice Programme, Police Reforms, Poverty Alleviation Programme and Political Participation in the Democratic Structure.

The Policy is a statement of intent of the Government of Pakistan to specify its measures for the development and empowerment of women. With the Policy providing the guidelines, this Ministry will ensure within the overall operating framework of the Government that the gender perspective is reflected in all national policies and plans.

Following are the visions of the policy:

In accordance with the vision of the Quaid-e-Azam, achievement of: gender equity and equality; social, political and economic empowerment of all Pakistani women at all levels; a just, humane and democratic society; economic prosperity through sustainable development; Goal Empowerment of Pakistani women, irrespective of caste, creed, religion, or other consideration for the realization of their full potential in all spheres of life, especially social, economic, personal and political and in keeping with our Islamic way of life.

Following are the aims and objectives of this policy:

To remove inequities and imbalances in all sectors of socio-economic development and to ensure women's equal access to all development benefits and social services.

To ensure the participation of women as equal partners in national development & decision-making processes in the community and society.

To ensure the full participation of women in all political processes and to enhance women's representation in all elective bodies.

To safeguard and ensure the protection of women's human rights including economic, legal, political and social rights, especially the rights of minority women, rural and poor women, girls & women with disabilities, elderly women and women in vulnerable circumstances and situations.

To provide women and girls access to quality health care services and all other pre-requisites to enjoying full health, including reproductive and mental health.

To expeditiously and substantially enhance women's literacy rates, improve attainment levels of girls and women at all levels of education (both academic and professional) to reduce the gender gap, and to reorient existing curricula by making them gender sensitive.

To provide equality of opportunity and to create space for women to realize their full potential.

Following are the guiding principles of this policy:

The Constitutional guarantees and accession to international instruments on human rights, as the reiteration of the Islamic principles of justice and equality.

Non-discrimination and gender equity at all levels.

Priority to the poorest of the poor, viz. women, especially in rural and isolated areas; girls and women in vulnerable situations/circumstances.

Recognition of the value of women's worth and work and their contribution in all spheres of life.

Women as equal partners in development and agents of change in economic, social and political processes.

The universally recognized rights and responsibility-based approach.

Following are the key policy measures:

Ensuring that government agencies adopt a gender sensitive approach to development in preparing needs based, participatory and implementable programmes and projects. Gender sensitization to be institutionalized and integrated into all sectors of development and to include the private sector as well.

Developing multi-sectoral and inter-disciplinary approaches for women's development, with horizontal and vertical linkages at every level.

Mainstreaming gender issues through integration into all sectors of national development

Eliminating all negative social practices.

Following are the sectors of policy deals with social empowerment of Women:

Education sector: As per the 1998 census, female literacy rates remain low at 32.6%. Although enrollment of girls has increased at a higher rate at all levels, their participation rate is much lower so that gender gaps continue to persist. And while participation rates of girls in urban areas have increased due to a policy of co-education at the primary level, high drop out rates beyond primary persist as a result of lack of opportunities, mobility issues as well as traditions and cultural norms constraining the access of girls and women (especially in the rural areas), to higher education.

To address these problems measures to be taken are:

Placing emphasis on primary school enrollment and on secondary schooling for girls through provision of scholarships and subsidies for girls education to low income households, equality of access and quality education for girls to narrow the existing gender gap, revision of curricula and text books at all educational levels for gender sensitization and provision of vocational and skills training, particularly in Information Technology. Affirming Government's Education Policy (under Education Sector Reforms) of Education for All and provisions and recommendations for compulsory primary education, incentive scheme for girls including improved input through female teacher training.

Health:

Pakistan's maternal mortality rate continues to be amongst the highest in the world. It is estimated that for every woman who dies, approximately 16 survive with chronic and long drawn out reproductive tract diseases. Advocacy and implementation of the life cycle approach, with improved health care and nutrition programmes for girls and women, promotion of ante and post - natal care, and enhanced provision of emergency obstetric care, curbing the spread of HIV/AIDs, remain a national challenge to better health.

The following measures will be taken to address the issues related to women's health:

Affirming the Government's Health Policy for All that underscores the emphasis for preventive and affordable primary health care provision for people, in particular reproductive health services for women;

Strengthening of basic health facilities for emergency obstetric care services at Tehsil/district levels to reduce women's morbidity and mortality rates and addressing the spread of HIV/Aids and drug abuse, through setting up of counselling and rehabilitation clinics.

Ensuring provision of quality health cover including for the mental health and well-being of women in line with the recommendations outlined in the ICPD Programme of Action. Ensuring reproductive health rights by involving men, women and adolescents, through non-coercive measures for family planning and promoting the small family norm in recognition of the principle of population stabilization through the adoption of a rights - based approach.

Law and Access to Justice:

Women are prevented from enjoying existing rights because of the prevalence of negative customary practices and attitudes; a general ignorance about rights and poor access to, and procedural problems in the justice system, and a generally poor implementation of the law. Other rights are denied through an absence of law. Moreover, affirmative provisions of the Constitution are seldom implemented to establish real and substantial equality. Consequently urgent action is needed to start addressing the multiple challenges in this area.

Key policy measures to be undertaken are:

Eliminating negative customary practices by increasing knowledge of women's existing rights under the law and of law itself, to access judicial relief and redress. Ensuring effective implementation and the enforcement of existing rights. Removing discrimination through legal reforms. Promoting women's access to justice by providing legal aid, assistance and counselling. An overall policy measure would be that, the Ministry of Law, Justice & Parliamentary Affairs, The Pakistan Law Commission, and the National Commission on the Status of Women shall review all Laws and formulate new legislation wherever needed.

Violence Against Women:

Violence against women plagues all societies and needs to be eliminated in all its forms. All space must be made safe for women and girls in the family, workplace, other private and public institutions including in police stations, lock-ups and jails, and public spaces in general. Violence against women persists because of cultural norms and attitudes that condone such acts, inadequate laws and access to shelters that fail to protect women from violence and/or to provide relief and justice to survivors of violence. Therefore, measures to address this issue are:

Adopting a zero tolerance policy regarding violence against women Declaring 'honour killings' as murder Reviewing and revising police and medico-legal procedures Introducing positive legislation on domestic violence and reform. Reviewing government policies for women's shelters, and improving shelters for women in the public and private sectors and promoting direct interaction and cooperation of all institutions/departments. Establishing family protection programmes at district level that provide women legal and psychological counselling and referrals to medical and legal aid mechanisms. Undertaking police reforms to increase the number of women in the police. Providing training to them and increasing women's sections in all police-stations which are fully equipped to deal with cases by having legal and medical officers and required facilities. Sensitizing all the police force on issues of violence against women.

Women in the Family & Community:

The family is the basic unit of society and women play a critical role by contributing to its welfare and to the development of society as a whole. However the importance of women's role in the family and society is neither fully recognized nor appreciated. Socially prescribed roles of women become a basis for discrimination and restrict the full participation of women in society. Women in Pakistan are especially disadvantaged by their lack of decision-making within the family and community, and restricted mobility that obstructs access to services.

To address these issues, the following measures are proposed:

Enabling women's access to all forms of information, resources, services and decision-making. Providing transport to facilitate access to basic facilities Upholding and ensuring women's right to inheritance and share in all kinds of joint property and financial rights in marriage. Enhancing the role of the media as a means of information, education and communication on women's issues and for a positive portrayal of women in all media. Initiating awareness campaigns - especially in the media and in schools through textbooks - to promote the positive benefits of an equal sharing of responsibilities, decision-making and power between family women and men inside and outside the home with focus on gender sensitive men and caring fathers and husbands. Encourage and further strengthen women's active participation in peace and conflict-resolution at all levels of society. Maximize for the benefit of society on women's concern for a sustainable environment, notably their efforts to ensure healthy food, clean water and air for future generations.

The Girl Child:

Girls in general suffer due to social conditions, from low self - esteem, minimal awareness of rights, very few opportunities (inadequate educational systems) and limited aspirations.

To improve the situation of the girl child the following measures will be undertaken:

Enabling girls without exception (including those with disabilities) to develop their full potential and skills through equal access to education and training, nutrition, physical and mental health care and related information and services in line with Pakistan's own national vision and its commitment at regional (SAARC) and international (UN) level.

Following are the sectors of policy deals with the economic empowerment of women:

Though women are an essential part of the country's economy, their share in economic benefits, opportunities and access to resources is not proportionate to their share in the population. Furthermore, increasing poverty as a result of structural adjustment programmes and globalization, disproportionately impacts women.

The following key policy measures are therefore to be undertaken:

Poverty:

Affirming government policies for poverty alleviation of the poorest of the poor, in particular women and endorses the provision of safety nets, food support schemes, and of provision of funds through Zakat. Providing adequate relief and safety measures to alleviate the disproportionate impact of poverty on women by ensuring access of poor rural women to land, agricultural and livestock extension services and support mechanisms and facilities Creating access to affordable housing schemes for women and promoting equality and the empowerment of women in all housing activities as espoused in the Government's Housing Policy 2001.

Access to Credit:

Providing women easy access to micro-credit especially through available windows such as Pakistan Poverty Alleviation Fund (PPAF); Rural Support Programmes (RSPs); First Women Bank (FWB); Agricultural Development Bank (ADB); Khushali Bank. Ensuring that women in general and female headed households, women bread earners, and women with disability in particular, have priority in accessing credit on soft terms from FWB and the Khushali Banks and other financial institutions for setting up their business, for buying properties, and for house building.

Remunerated Work:

Increasing women's capacity to earn by improving Access to sources of livelihood, particularly in agriculture and livestock production. Providing equal opportunities for women in remunerated employment which also accommodate women-oriented work patterns. Improving facilities for the education, training and skills development for women, to enter and re-enter the labour force, including special arrangements, as specified in the draft Labour Policy for women relatives of workers. Ensuring appropriate legislation, including the following measures as proposed in the draft Labour Policy. Give effect to the ILO Convention 100 ratified by Pakistan in 2001 by enacting a law to ensure equal remuneration for men and women for work of equal value. Undertake measures to make work places conducive for women workers so they can work without fear of discrimination and harassment. Enact a law and guidelines to provide protection against sexual harassment at the workplace and relief/remedy in cases where it occurs. Providing special courses for women in entrepreneurial skills to assist and engage them to establish their own small-scale enterprises.

Women in the Rural Economy and Informal Sector:

Recognizing, counting and making visible women's real economic contribution and productivity in both the formal and informal sectors of the economy in national economic indicators. Formally recognizing women working in the rural economy and the informal sector as workers and taking measures to ensure healthy and safe conditions of work.

Sustainable Development:

Maintaining natural resources to sustain livelihoods is the fundamental principle of sustainable development. Pakistan's natural resource base is rapidly depleting due to poor management and overuse and negatively impacting women in the process, particularly rural women, who depend on the available natural resources (water, fuel, fodder, herbs) for fulfilling their families livelihood needs. Urgent measures are therefore required in this area:

Including women from the tiers of local government to the national level in key decision-making bodies pertaining to the environment specially the Pakistan Environment Protection Council. Mandatory assessment of the impact of development and environment projects, programmes and policies on women. Providing training, skills and information to women in natural resource management including soil conservation, water, forestry, mangroves and rangeland management. Affirming and supporting the policies and principles related to women enunciated by the National Conservation Strategy and the Provincial Conservation Strategies of NWFP and Balochistan. Highlighting the close link between women and the environment through supporting and initiating research in order to develop appropriate programmes and policies to address women's needs in this sector. Conserving women's indigenous knowledge related traditional medicines, natural resource management practices, local foods and food preservation techniques.

Following are the sectors of policy deals with the political empowerment of women:

Power & Decision-Making:

A positive step in this direction has been taken by the present Government through the introduction of the reservation of 33% seats in the local councils on the basis of joint and direct elections and more than twice the number of reserved seats for women at the national and provincial levels. The following additional key measures are to be adopted:

Ensuring effective implementation of existing provisions.

Removing hurdles to women's political participation by effective implementation of existing legal provisions, and by removing procedural obstacles.

Strengthening women in political decision making positions by providing training supervision/support and defining their authority and through engaging male colleagues in the development of gender equality in decision-making.

Mandating the inclusion of women through merit in all decision-making bodies of the executive and judicial organs of the state at the federal, provincial and local/district levels, and by taking measures to remove obstacles in women's access to power and decision-making in the family, community and society, including on important global issues related to peace, conflict, resolution and presentations of a sustainable environment.

Note: All measures outlined above for the social, economic and political empowerment of women will equally apply to elderly women, women and girls with disabilities and other marginalized groups.

Power & Decision-Making:

A positive step in this direction has been taken by the present Government through the introduction of the reservation of 33% seats in the local councils on the basis of joint and direct elections and more than twice the number of reserved seats for women at the national and provincial levels. The following additional key measures are to be adopted:

Ensuring effective implementation of existing provisions.

Removing hurdles to women's political participation by effective implementation of existing legal provisions, and by removing procedural obstacles.

Strengthening women in political decision making positions by providing training supervision/support and defining their authority and through engaging male colleagues in the development of gender equality in decision-making.

Mandating the inclusion of women through merit in all decision-making bodies of the executive and judicial organs of the state at the federal, provincial and local/district levels, and by taking measures to remove obstacles in women's access to power and decision-making in the family, community and society, including on important global issues related to peace, conflict, resolution and presentations of a sustainable environment.

Note: All measures outlined above for the social, economic and political empowerment of women will equally apply to elderly women, women and girls with disabilities and other marginalized groups.

Policy Implementation:

Implementation of the national policy for development and empowerment of women will be the responsibility of the GOP, through its line Ministries and Provincial Departments.

Institutional Arrangements/Mechanisms.

Ministry of Women Development (MoWD):

The Ministry of Women Development (MoWD) was established with a clear mandate of formulating policies and to recommend legislation to meet the specific needs of women creating an adequate infrastructure to implement the National Policy for Women's Development and Empowerment will necessitate functioning of a strong and revitalized Ministry for Women's Development. The Ministry will be provided sufficient human and financial resources in order to play an effective role as catalyst and for coordinating and monitoring. As the focal machinery, MoWD will be strengthened and structured to ensure effective gender mainstreaming at all levels. The MoWD will regularly brief Cabinet on progress of implementation of policy and facilitate gender sensitization and training programmes for all other Ministries. Women Development Departments (WDDs) at provincial & district levels, to do the same.

MoWD will serve as the repository of information on women and will disseminate the same through linkages with various research and academic institutions, in particular, University based Women Study Departments.

NCSW:

The role of the National Commission on the Status of Women (NCSW) will be as stipulated in Ordinance NO. XXVI of 2000 paras 7a-f

Coordination:

As the national focal machinery/point, MoWD will have linkages with other line ministries at Federal level through designated focal points. At the provincial and district levels, MoWD will coordinate implementation through its departments and through designated focal points of other line departments including local government. It will also facilitate implementation through public/ private sector coordination mechanism especially with NGOs.

For monitoring impact of effective policy implementation, MoWD will coordinate with the Federal Bureau of Statistics, research and academic institutions, to ensure collection of accurate information, desegregated by gender, age, socio-economic class and region and its analysis by relevant agencies

Monitoring:

As the focal Ministry and focal departments, the MOWD and the WDDs will be the primary monitoring, review & coordinating bodies.

Following is the National Plan of Action (NPA) of the policy:
The MoWD, SW&SE in collaboration with UNDP under Gender Equality Umbrella Project (GEUP) has reviewed the implementation of Beijing Declaration and Platform of Action. The review has attempted to collate and synthesize all official reviews of the National Plan of Action (NPA) for implementation process through an analysis of the government approach and efforts since the Beijing Conference 1995. The review, inter-alia, has taken into account the inputs received from the concerned Ministries / Divisions, provincial Women Development Departments and Planning and Development Department, Northern Areas.

The NPA for Women set out in twelve (12) areas of concern, establishes a set of priority action formulated to help achieve the agenda for the empowerment of women in Pakistan. Prepared on the basis of national participatory process, involving Federal and Provincial Governments, NGOs, Women Organizations and individual experts the NPA aims to facilitate women's participation an all spheres of life besides ensuring protection of women's rights within the family and the society. NPA twelve (12) areas of concern are as under:-

Women and Poverty; Education and Training of Women; Women and Health; Violence Against Women; Women and Armed Conflict; Women and Economy; Women in Power and Decision-making; Institutional mechanisms for the Advancement of Women; Human Rights of Women; Women and Media; Women and Environment; The Girl Child.

Appendix C

Ministry of Women Development, Social Welfare and Special Education
Government of Pakistan

Questionnaire on the Implementation of the Beijing Platform for Action[63]

Critical Areas of Concern	Examples of successful policies, programmes and projects to implement the critical areas of concern of the Beijing Platform for Action (Indicate any targets and strategies set and related achievements)	Examples of obstacles encountered/lessons learnt	Commitment to further action/new initiatives
Women and poverty	➤ In order to involve women in productive economic activities, including exports, the Ministry is moving forward on a broad-based programme in collaboration with the private sector. ➤ An Export Trade House and Display Centre each has been established at Lahore and Islamabad. Similar ventures are proposed at Karachi, Muzaffarabad and other major cities. ➤ To facilitate women entrepreneurs in their business activities both local and foreign, Business Centres in collaboration with the First Women Bank Limited (FWBL) have been established at Islamabad, Lahore and Karachi. Similar Centres are planned for Quetta, Peshawar and other major cities. ➤ The First Women Bank Limited (FWBL) is operating its 38 branches to facilitate banking and micro-credit schemes for women. ➤ Regional Development Finance Corporation (RDFC) has opened its credit line to fund projects for women. ➤ The Ministry has funded 266 Vocational Training Centres in the public and private sectors, including AJandK. The Ministry now intends to convert these vocational Centres into	Women's access to micro credit through existing public and private sectors windows is necessary. There are only two major formal sources of micro credit for women i.e. First Women Bank and ADBP.	➤ Pakistan Poverty Alleviation Fund established by the Government of Pakistan for poverty alleviation will be playing the major role in micro credit. ➤ State Bank of Pakistan has been requested to direct commercial banks, ADBP and SBFC to allocate 5% of their resources for micro credit and 30% of which should go to women for small business. ➤ Women will also be given representation on National Credit Consultative Council.

[63] This material was provided to the Division for the Advancement of Women by the Government of Pakistan in response to the Secretary General's questionnaire on implementation of the Beijing Platform for Action. This appendix provides only that material which is related to only two areas that is "Women and Poverty" and "Women and the Economy".

Area	Achievements	Issues	Recommendations
	Production and Display Centres. Initially, Training Centres, Training Centres functioning in major cities are being selected for this up-gradation. ➤ MoWD has provided a credit line of Rs. 48 million to First Women Bank. These loans are utilized in boutique and tailoring, beauty parlours at small scale, bakeries, catering, tuition centers, grocery and general stores and carpet weaving in urban areas. In rural areas these are utilized in cultivation, poultry, dairy and fish farming, livestock, general stores, tailoring etc. Disbursement for Rs. 142.146 million has created employment for 21,606 women.		
Women and the Economy	➤ Five per cent quota has been allocated in Employment in Provincial and Federal Government Departments, autonomous bodies and attached Departments. ➤ Industrial Homes have been established by MoWD. ➤ Export Trade Houses have ben established in major cities. ➤ MoWD has provided a credit line of Rs. 48 million to First Women Bank, Rs. 30 million in 1991 and Rs. 18 million in 1993. ➤ Working Women Hostels have been established by MoWD. ➤ Establishment of Day Care Centres. ➤➤ 12 separate enclosure for women in open markets have been set up in Weekly Bazaars for economic empowerment of women and to encourage women entrepreneurs to undertake income generating activities for their betterment.	➤ Shortage of educational and training facilities. ➤ Shortage of provision of necessary facilities to working women in the public and private sector. ➤ Shortage of infrastructure. ➤ Role of middleman. ➤ Lack of awareness about marketing skills.	➤ Inclusion of Women's Study as a subject at Graduate and postgraduate level. ➤ Income generating skill development centers have been established. ➤ Highlighting of the benefits of women in all programmes/PC-Is of concerned ministries.

Appendix D

Submitted by the NGO Coordinating Committee for Beijing +5; two relevant areas are included out of 12 critical areas reported

C.1 Area of Concern: Women and Poverty

Good Initiatives	Obstacles	Emerging Trends	Future Actions	Gaps and Persistent Issues
NOTE Given the bleak economic situation, no good macro-level initiatives could be identified-micro initiatives identified cannot answer macro-needs.	Lack of political will to reorient macro-economic policies; Unclear/inappropriate priorities and mismanagement of existing resources.	Poverty levels increased to 35-38 %; Poverty of Opportunity Index increased to 44% in 1995.	Institute land reforms and land distribution and promote employment opportunities in necessary development schemes, ensuring women's employment opportunities and benefits, and expedite implementation of NPA with frequent review and monitoring.	Poor governance/lack of political will compounds problems of basic underlying macro-economic structure.
Poverty Alleviation Fund established.	Globalization, Structural Adjustment Programmes and IMF policies.	Poverty aggravated through Structural Adjustment Policies and globalization, while positive impact of safety-net measures not visible.	Increase public-private-NGO partnerships to enlarge, expand and replicate some of the successful NGO initiatives and pilot programmes over the past 5-10 years.	Fundamental gaps in process between intentions/documents and implementation, lack of interest, gaps between needs and resource allocations.
	A higher annual population than economic growth rate negates macro-level gains.	Increasing number of female headed households.	Allocate 30% for female headed households in all public and private sector land and housing programmes, ensure women are 50% of beneficiaries of all schemes.	Continued depletion of natural resources by unsustainable exploitation and misused eroding modes of sustenance for women.

C.2 Area of Concern: Women and the Economy

Good Initiatives	Obstacles	Emerging Trends	Future Actions	Gaps and Persistent Issues
NOTE Given the bleak economic situation, no good macro-level initiatives could be identified-micro initiatives identified cannot answer macro-needs.	Women's lack of access to all forms of resources and opportunities.	Increasing number of women in labour market in the formal, informal and semi-formal sectors independent of planned policies.	Rethink, review and restructure macro-economic policies and eliminate Structural Adjustment Programmes by the State; Ensure women are sufficiently represented in all economic policy-making bodies.	No reduction (rather increase in) levels of poverty (from 25-30% to 35-38%).
Redefinition of work to include women's contribution as agricultural workers in Labour Force Survey.	Misdirected use of minimal available resources that promotes export-oriented activities, instead of addressing indigenous needs.	Increasing number of women-headed household mostly in marginalized tasks.	State to re-assume and fulfill its essential responsibility of providing basic needs for all sections of society, particularly women and other disadvantaged groups.	Women neither decision makers not addressed in macro-level economic planning and policy making.
Micro-credit schemes and self-employment for women by public sector banks (FWBL and UBL) and NGOs.	No mechanism to assist women entrepreneurs beyond micro-level.	Increasing visible poverty, lack of access to basic needs, education/training and employment opportunities.	Create employment opportunities for women, increase appropriate skills training and credit facilities for women.	No legislative cover/recognition for majority of women in agriculture, informal and semi-formal sectors.

Appendix E
Project Research Team

Consultant

Mr. Nabeel A. Goheer

Project Coordinator

Ms. Uzma Ather

Enumerators in Lahore

Ms. Ameena Saddiqui MA (Sociology)

Ms. Zareen MA (Mass Communications)

Ms. Nosheen Zafar MA (Social Work)

Ms. Saadia Saleem MA (Social work)

Ms. Maryam Nakai MA (Sociology)

Ms. Sara Kalim MA (Sociology)

Enumerators in Rawalpindi/ICT

Ms. Naadia Rathore Msc (Psychology)

Mrs. Ghazala Sheraz BA (Hons)

Ms. Najeeha B.A

Ms. Riffat B.A

Ms. Shabana B.A

Data Processing

Mr. Khawaja Ahsan Tayyeb

Mr. Mohammad Sarwar

Appendix F

Research Questionnaire

Improving the Bargaining Power of Women Entrepreneurs

Date of interview:	dd_____ mm_____ yy_____
Interviewer's name:	

QUALITY CONTROL *[to be filled in by supervisor after interview]*		Corrected	Yes	No
Checked by:				
Date checked:				
City:				

RESPONDENT CRITERIA (to be asked by interviewer prior interview)

Please ensure that the respondent meets the following criteria by asking:	Yes	No
Do you own/Lion shareholder/manager of this business?	1	2
Do you have 5 or more than 5 employees in your business	1	2
Do you operate this business from dedicated business premises other than your residence	1	2

Part 1. Profile of the Entrepreneur

1.1 (Show Card) **Which age bracket are you in?**

Less than 20	1
20-39	2
40-49	3
50-59	4
60-above	5

1.2 (Show Card) **What is the level of your education?**

Postgraduate	1
Graduate/Vocational	2
Secondary/Primary	3
No formal education	4

1.3 (Show Card) **what is the highest level of education completed by your mother?**

Postgraduate	1
Graduate/Vocational	2
Secondary/Primary	3
Just Literate	4
No formal education	5

1.4 (Show Card) **what is the highest level of education completed by your father?**

Postgraduate	1
Graduate/Vocational	2
Secondary/Primary	3
Just Literate	4
No formal education	5

1.5 **What is your marital status? (Show card)**

Single	1 (Go to 1.9)
Married	2
Separated	3
Divorced	4
Widowed	5

1.6 **Do you have Children?**

Yes	1
No	2 (Go to 1.9)

1.7 **How many children do you have (if yes to 1.8)?**

Girl/(s) -----------	Boy/(s) -----------

1.8   What are the ages of your children?

Girl/(s)	Boy/(s)
1.	1.
2.	2.
3.	3.
4.	4.

1.9   What kind of family structure are you living in? (Please explain the terms to the entrepreneur)

Nuclear family[64]	1
Extended Family[65]	2
Alone	3 (go to 1.11)
Other (specify)	4

(Ask this question from respondents who are married according to Q 1.5)

1.10   (Show card) what is the highest level of education completed by your spouse?

Postgraduate	1
Graduate/Vocational	2
Secondary/Primary	3
Just Literate	4
No formal education	5

1.11   What were you doing immediately before starting this business? (Get a single response)

Student	1
Unemployed	2
Employed	3
House wife	4
Another business (specify)	5
Other (Specify)	6

1.12   Did you had any prior work experience relating to this business? (Please explain)

Yes-Substantial	1
Very little	2
No-Started from scratch	3

1.13   Did you undergo any specific training or education to start/scale up this business?

MBA/Accounting/Professional Training	1
Short Computer Course	2
Short Management Course	3
Small Business Course	4
Technical Training (specify)	5
Certificate course (specify)	6
Diploma (specify)	7
Other (specify)	8
None	9

---

[64] Husband, wife and unmarried children.
[65] Nuclear family and other relatives.

1.14 **(Show Card) What computer skills do you have?** (Multiple Response)

I can compose a letter	1
I can use email and Internet	2
I can use spreadsheets and prepare power point presentation	3
My computer skills are more than 1, 2 and 3 above	4
No I cannot use a computer	0

1.15 **Who established this business?**

Already established by family	1 (If yes-specify father, mother etc.)
Myself	2
Myself and my family	3 (If yes-ask which person in the family)
Myself and my friends	4
Somebody else (specify)	5 (If yes — go to 1.19)

1.16 **What were the most important motivating factors to start this business?** (Ask 1.16, 1.17, and 1.18 if the answer to 1.15 is <u>not</u> 1 and 5)

1.
2.
3.

1.17 **Please tell the major factors that were helpful in starting this business?**

1.
2.
3.

1.18 **Were there any problems that you faced specifically as a women entrepreneur in starting this business?**

1.19 **Do you want your business to grow?**

Yes: I want my business to grow	1
I want my business to remain almost like it is now	2
No: I want my business to grow	3

1.20 **What are the most important factors that can help your business to grow?** (Up to 3)

1.
2.
3.

1.21 **What are the most significant barriers in the growth of your business?** (Up to 3)

1.
2.
3.

Part 2. Profile of the Enterprise
Part 2.1: General

2.1.22 **What is the size of the enterprise in terms of number of employees?**

Micro (5-9)	
Small (10-35)	
Medium (36-99)	

2.1.23 **What kind of business is this?**

Trade	1
Manufacturing	2
Service	3
Other (specify)	4

2.1.24 **What are the main products/ services of your business?**

2.1.25 **Where are the major operations of this business located?**

City/Town:

2.1.26 **When this business was established?**

Year:

2.1.27 **What is the legal status of your business?** (Read out and get single response)

Single Owner/Sole Proprietor	1
Partnership (Registered)	2
Partnership (Unregistered)	3
Private Company	4
Public Company	5
Cooperative Society/NGO	6
Other (specify)	7

2.1.28 **Do you own the business premises?**

Own	1
Rented	2
Other (specify)	3

2.1.29   What is your management style?

Hierarchical[66]	1
Consensus based[67]	2
Other (specify)	3

2.1.30   What is the most important factor in adopting this management style? (Select one)

It is more effective	1
It is more productive	2
It suits our culture	3
Other (specify)	4

2.1.31   Do you have a personal bank account?

Yes	1
No	2

2.1.32   Do you have a separate bank account (other than your personal account) for this business?

Yes	1
No	2

2.1.33   How many employees do you have?

	Women	Men
Full Time		
Part Time		
Paid Family Member		
Unpaid Family Member		

2.1.34   Has your business grown (experienced a positive change in sales etc.) in the past one year?

Phenomenal Growth	1
Normal Growth	2
Stay the same	3
Negative growth	4
Drastic negative growth	5

---

[66] Decisions are made by the top management and communicated by the middle management to the junior management.
[67] Decisions include everybody and made through consultation.

2.1.35   What are your long-term plans for your business?

Continue/expand present business	1
Change to another line of business	2
Leave and take up wage employment	3
Pass the business onto someone else in my family	4
Sell the business	5
Hire a manager	6
Retire	7
Other (specify)	8

2.1.36   How do you expect to continue your business over the next year?

(Do NOT read out; multi-mention: ask this question only if the respondent has answered 'Continue with present business' in questions 2.1.35)

	Yes	No
No changes planned	1	2
Make new investments in the business	1	2
Expand/improve the business		
Increase the number of workers	1	2
Decrease the number of workers	1	2
Expand the range of products/services	1	2
Reduce the range of products/services	1	2
Don't know	1	2
Other (specify)	1	2

2.1.37   How do you expect your business to perform in the next three years, compared to how it did in the past three years? *(Read out: single mention)*

Very good	1
Good	2
OK	3
Poor	4
Very Poor	5

2.1.38   What is your opinion on _____(attribute mentioned below) on 5 point rating scale
          from +2 to – 2 where +2 means Strongly Agree
          and –2 means Strongly Disagree with this statement (Show Card) ?

	+2 Strongly Agree	+1 Agree	0 Can't say anything	-1 Disagree	-2 Strongly Disagree
The overall environment for women entrepreneurs is good					
Family and social commitments are growing					
Government support to women entrepreneurs is increasing					
The costs of running business are increasing					
Access to finance and credit for women entrepreneurs is increasing.					
Access to women business support networks is increasing					
Market for women entrepreneurs is expanding					
Business know how of women entrepreneurs is increasing					
Technical skills of women entrepreneurs are increasing					

2.1.39   How do you obtain orders for your products and services?

2.1.40   Who takes these orders?

Myself   1
Marketing staffs (specify male/female)   2
Other (specify)   3

2.1.41   As a women entrepreneur do you feel any constraints in getting these orders?

Yes (specify)   1
No   2

2.1.42   How do you get your products/services to the market?

Myself   1
Marketing staffs (specify male/female)   2
Other (specify)   3

2.1.43   Who delivers your products/services to the market?

Myself   1
Marketing staffs (specify male/female)   2
Other (specify)   3

2.1.44   As a women entrepreneur do you feel any constraints in delivery of your products/services?

Yes (specify)   1
No   2

2.1.45   Which one of the following is your largest market? (Read out, Single Response)

Local markets	1
Regional or provincial markets	2
National markets	3
International markets	4
Other (specify)	5

2.1.46   What is the mode of marketing?

Managed by the company herself	1
Through an intermediary	2
Production is based on demand only	3
Sold to retailers	4
Others (Specify)	5

2.1.47   Have you always sold in the same markets?

Yes	1
No	2

2.1.48   Which new markets are you now operating in?
         (Ask this question if the answer is No in 2.1.47)

2.1.49   What are three major marketing constraints of your business? (Please explain)

1. ---

2. ---

3. ---

2.1.50   What promotional events or exhibitions have you participated in over the last three years?

1.
2.
3.

2.1.51   Do you have a web site to promote/market your business?

Yes	1
No	2
We are in the process of developing	3

2.1.52   Have you made any technology improvement in your business in the past one-year and how?
         (Read out and ask how if the response is 1, 2 or 3)

Substantial	1
Moderate	2
Marginal	3
Not at all	4

2.1.53   What kind of technology is helpful for your business and how?

Type of Technology	How it can help the business

2.1.54   Do you happen to know any of the following institutions and their purpose?

PCSIR (Pakistan Council for Scientific and Industrial Research)	1
STEDEC (Scientific and Technological Development Corporation)	2
PITAC (Pakistan Industrial and Technical Assistance Center)	3
NPO (National Productivity Organization)	4
PVTC (Punjab Vocational Training Council)	5
TEVTA (Technical Education and Vocational Training Authority)	6
None	7

2.1.55   Do you think that Pakistan's accession to WTO is going to change your business in any of the following ways?

Favorably	1
Moderately	2
Drastically	3
Have no idea	4

2.1.56   Are you a member of any of the following organizations? (Read out, multiple response)

Chamber of Commerce and Industry	1
Related Business Organization	2
Any Networking Group	3
Pakistan Association of Women Entrepreneurs	4
Export Promotion Bureau	5
Others (Specify)	6
None	7

2.1.57   Have you received any help from any government or private agency in the last three years?

Yes	1 (What kind of help? Please explain)
No	2

82

2.2.58   Are there some family members who help you in running this business? (Please specify sex)

Nobody	1
Close Blood Relations (father, mother, brother, sister etc.)	2
Relatives from in-laws (husband, mother in law etc.)	3
Other relatives/friends	4

2.2.59   How many family members are there in your management team (if yes in 2.2.58)?

Management Staff (total)	Family Members		Others	
	Male:	Female	Male:	Female:

2.2.60   How many family members are there in your supervisory staff?

Supervisory Staff (total)	Family Members		Others	
	Male:	Female	Male:	Female:

2.2.61   How many family members are there as workers?

Workers (total)	Family Members		Others	
	Male:	Female	Male:	Female:

2.2.62   What percentage of your monthly income from this business contributes to your total Household Income? (Read out, single response)

None	1
Up to 25%	2
Up to 50%	3
More than 50%	4

2.2.63   What percentage of your profit is reinvested in this business? (Read out, single response)

None	1
Up to 25%	2
Up to 50%	3
More than 50%	4

2.2.64   Who do you normally ask for advice on business problems?

Family Member (Please specify)	1
Relative/ Friend (Please specify)	2
General Manager/Director/Employee	3
Other (specify)	4

2.2.65   Who takes the final decision regarding investments in machinery/other fixed assets?

2.2.66   **How do you take this decision?** (Read out from the card)

On the basis of my own judgement	1
In consultation with a family member (specify)	2
In consultation with a relative/friend (specify)	3
In consultation with General Manager/Director/Employee	4
Other (specify)	5

2.2.67   **Who decides about new recruitment in the business?**

2.2.68   **How do you decide about new recruitment in the business?**

My own judgement	1
In consultation with a family member (specify)	2
In consultation with a relative/friend (specify)	3
In consultation with General Manager/Director/Employee (specify)	4
Other (specify)	5

2.2.69   **Who takes final decisions regarding marketing and sales?**

2.2.70   **Who is responsible in your business for making/maintaining Public contacts (Other than Marketing)?**

2.2.71   **Who signs legal documents like business contracts etc.?**

2.2.72   **What is the average number of hours/day that you spend for the business?**

2.2.73   **What is the average number of hours/day that you spend with the family/ household?**

2.2.74   **How many other members of the family contribute to the household income (specify number and gender)?**

Part 3. Business Environment
3.1 Government Policies/Regulations and Institutions

3.1.75   Are you cognizant of the following policies of the government?

	Yes	No
Policies by the Board of Investment that provide incentives for new and existing investments		
Policies of the Ministry of Commerce and Industry for trade and Export Promotion		
Policies of the Ministry of Finance like income and sales tax concessions		
Policies of the State Bank of Pakistan for concessional loans		
SROs issued by the Central Bureau of Revenue for tariff concessions		
Policies of the Ministry of Labour that entail labour related regulations		

3.1.76   Do you think that the present policy environment discriminates against the women entrepreneurs?

Yes (how?)	1
No (how?)	2
Neutral (It is neither positively nor negatively biased)	3
No opinion	4

3.1.77   What changes in the government policies are needed to promote women Entrepreneurs?

3.1.78   (Show Round card) What area of government regulation do you think is the most difficult to comply with ? Second most difficult? Third, Fourth and Fifth ?

Labour
Tax
Trade
Licensing
Business
Other (specify)

3.1.79   (Show Round Card) which was the most important factor that have <u>NEGATIVELY</u> affected your business in the recent past (mark 1 in the box), Also assign 2, 3, 4, 5, and 6 as second, third, fourth, fifth, and sixth factors respectively?

Regulatory Environment (government policies, regulations and institutions)
Law and Order situation
Lack of adequate financing facilities
Lack of business development services (management, marketing, etc)
Economic slowdown
Other (Specify)

3.1.80 (Show Round Card) which was the most important factor that have <u>POSITIVELY</u> affected your business in the recent past (mark 1 in the box), Also assign 2, 3, 4, 5, and 6 as second, third, fourth, fifth, and sixth factors respectively?

Regulatory Environment (government policies, regulations and institutions)
Law and order situation
Adequate financing facilities
Business development services (management, marketing, etc)
Economic growth
Other (Specify)

3.1.81 (Show Round card) Which help by the Government is desired by you the most? Second? Third, Fourth, Fifth? (Rank the responses)

Lesser Government Regulations
Reduced Costs of Utility Inputs (Electricity, Gas etc)
Loans at Concessional rates of Interest
Business Development Services
Other (Please specify)

3.2 Finance

3.2.82   How did you finance your business at the start? (Multiple Response)

My own savings	1
Credit from the formal source	2
Credit from the Informal source (Friends and Family)	3
Somebody else invested	4
Other (specify)	5

3.2.83   Have you borrowed money for the business in the last three years?

No   1
Yes   2 (If Yes then ask source as following)

Formal Source		**Informal Source**	
Commercial Banks	1	Friend	1
Leasing Companies	2	Family	2
DFIs	3	Relative	3
PSIC	4	Money Lender	4
Other (specify)	5	Other (specify)	5

3.2.84   (If Formal Source then ask) How was Collateral managed ?

3.2.85   For what purpose did you borrow money (if yes in 3.2 86)?

Plant and Equipment Investment	1
Working Capital	2
Trade Finance	3
Real Estate	4
Other (specify)	5

3.2.86   What problems did you face in borrowing money (if answer is formal source in 3.2.86)?

Access to the Financial Institutions	1
Cumbersome procedures	2
High Interest Rates	3
Strict Terms and Conditions	4
Other (specify)	5

3.2.87   Do you think that being a woman is a major constraint in getting formal finance?

Yes	1
No	2

3.2.88   (If yes in 3.2.90 how?)

3.3 Non-Financial Services

3.3.89   Did you or your staff undergo any training in the last three years?

	(a) Self	(b)Staff
Yes	1	1
No	2	2 (Go to 3.3.90)

3.3.90   (If Yes for self) What kind of training did you get?

3.3.91   (If Yes for self) From where did you get that training?

3.3.92   (If Yes for staff) What kind of training your staff got?

3.3.93   (If Yes for staff) From where your staff got that training?

3.3.94   Was the training useful ?

	Self	**Staff**
Yes	1	1
No	2	2

3.3.95   Have you availed the following services from the Government/Private Institutions in the past three years?

	Government	**Private Institutes**
Management	1	1
Marketing	2	2
Software Development	3	3
E Marketing	4	4
Technology Development	5	5
Export-related Advice	6	6
Legal	7	7
Other (specify)	8	8

3.3.96   (Show Round card) Which is the most important factor for the growth of your business where you expect the Chamber of Commerce and Industry to extend help? Which is the second? Third, Fourth, Fifth, sixth? (Please prioritize)?

Networking
Marketing
Finance
Training (specify)
Legal
Other (specify)

3.3.97   (Show Round Card) Which is the most important factor for the growth of your business where you expect the Related Business Associations to extend help? Second? Third, Fourth, Fifth? (Please prioritize)?

Networking
Marketing
Finance
Training (specify)
Legal
Other (specify)

3.3.98 (Show Round card) Which is the most important factors for the growth of your business where you expect the Donors to extend help? Second, Third, Fourth, Fifth (Please prioritize)?

Networking
Marketing
Finance
Training (specify)
Legal
Other (specify)

3.3.99 Could you please list four non-financial business support services that are the most important for your business?

1.
2.
3.
4.

3.3.100 What do you think about the performance of existing women support organizations in terms of their out reach?

Good   1
Not so good   2
Bad   3
Do not know 4

3.3.101 How (in your opinion) this outreach can be improved?

3.3.102 What do you think about the performance of existing women support organizations in terms of the range of services that they provide?

Good   1
No so good   2
Bad   3
Do not know   4

3.3.103 How (in your opinion) this range of services can be improved?

3.3.104 Have you received help (non-financial) from the women support organization/(s) in the last three years?

Year	Type of Help	Name of the Organization

3.3.105 **What should be the role of Women Business Forums in Pakistan to help the women entrepreneurs in their business-related problems?**

3.3.106 **What do you think are the major business issues faced only by the woman entrepreneurs in Pakistan and not the male entrepreneurs?**

3.4 Social/Cultural

3.4.107 **Are you the first woman member of your family who started business?**

Yes	1
No	2

3.4.108 **What was the response of your family when you entered into this business?**

Very Supportive	1
Supportive	2
Indifferent	3
Non supportive	4
Reacted badly	5

3.4.109 **(Ask this question if the answer is 1 and 2 in 3.4.107) How your family was/is supportive?**

3.4.110 **(Ask this question if the answer is 4 and 5 in 3.4.107) What hindrances you are facing from your family?**

3.4.111   How did the business affect your family life and in what ways? (Specify)

Very Positively   1
Positively   2
Can't Say anything   3
Negatively   4
Very Negatively   5

3.4.112   What are social/cultural barriers that negatively affect your doing business in Pakistan?

1.
2.
3.

3.4.113   How do you think these barriers could be reduced/removed?

3.4.114   What are social/ cultural aspects that positively contribute to your doing business in Pakistan?
1.
2.
3.

3.4.115   How do you think that doing business has affected your social image in the society?

Improved   1
Remained the same   2
Worsened   3

3.4.116   What general comments you hear from society about your doing business?

Positive Comments:

Negative Comments:

**3.4.117   How do you think that the perceptions about women doing business are changing in the society?
What changes in the attitude of society you have noticed in the past three years?**

Significantly improved towards doing business   1   (Go to 3.4.115)
Improved   2   (Go to 3.4.115)
Can not say anything   3
Not Improved   4   (Go to 3.4.116)
Worsened   5   (Go to 3.4.116)

3.4.118   What positive improvement you have noticed in the social attitude?

3.4.119   What negative trends you have noticed in the social attitude?

Name of Enterprise: --

Name of Entrepreneur: ---

Qualification of Entrepreneur:--

Business address: ---

Contact:

Telephone: ---

Fax: ---

Email: ---

Website: --

What is the value of Productive assets — excluding land and building? (including raw material, stocks and machinery)

Up to Rs. 2,00,000.00	1
Rs. 200,001 to Rs. 2 Crore	2
Rs. 2 Crore to Rs. 4 Crore	3
More than 4 Crore*	4

Total investment:

Average Monthly Sales:

Thank you very much for your cooperation

Any Comments:

Appendix G

Study of Women Entrepreneurs (WE) in Pakistan (Terms of Reference): Improving the Bargaining Power of Women Entrepreneurs

The Government of Pakistan's policy documents and other research has increasingly been articulating that the micro and small enterprise (MSE) is one of the sectors that is essential for growth and economic revival. This is consistent with many other countries throughout the world. At present 40 per cent of Pakistan's GDP is attributed to the broader Micro, Small and Medium Enterprise sector. The female labour force participation stands at 13.6 per cent, the bulk of which is in the informal sector, varying from home-based units to micro and small enterprises.

Increasingly, women-owned enterprises are being viewed, not simply as vehicles for poverty alleviation, but rather as business units in their own right, contributing to the creation of new jobs (68) and developing their own distinctive styles of management and networking. The ILO believes that the creation of decent jobs for women and men is the most significant and positive solution for reducing poverty. However, even in the developed world some barriers remain that inhibit the potential of women entrepreneurs to develop and grow, and contribute fully to economic development. In Pakistan, through this action research activity the ILO wants to ensure that such barriers do not prevent the creation and expansion of women-owned enterprises.

In recent years in Pakistan there has also been a gradual growth of support initiatives in both the public and private sectors, mainly to promote enterprise development. Correspondingly, activities to promote women's entrepreneurship have also been initiated by the Government, donors and international agencies, and NGOs and CBOs. Successful micro-finance and micro-credit schemes have been ongoing for some years now, such as the First Women's Bank, Bank of Khyber, Aga Khan AKRSP, National Rural Support Programmes (NRSPs) and, more recently the Khushali Bank. Several of these have also contributed to supporting women's enterprise development. These schemes provide micro-credit to women as part of a wider contribution to poverty reduction and gender and development (GAD) objectives. There have also been a number of non-financial support interventions in areas of business development services (BDS), such as skills training, entrepreneurship training, and opportunity identification, carried out by donor-assisted projects, as well as by the ILO in collaboration with the Employers' Federation of Pakistan.

In addition, as a result of these recent support initiatives, it is now felt that there is a considerable amount of unrecorded information, and experiences and lessons available on the constraints and problems. Similarly, there is much information on the opportunities and enabling factors for the growth of women entrepreneurs, the various successes and failures, and emerging national "good practice" programmes and projects. However, little of this information is available in the public domain. In order to formulate and develop workable, effective, targeted and cost-efficient strategies, it is necessary to examine the factors influencing women entrepreneurs in their successes and failures, with a view to assisting women entrepreneurs in upscaling and increasing their negotiation skills and bargaining power.

Review of the current situation: There is a variety of experiences arising from the support provided to WE in Pakistan, but these experiences have not been documented and analyzed. Thus, information is lacking on:
- the quality of the existing support programs (their impact, outreach);
- the extent to which they serve the actual demand (demand-orientation); and
- the nature of the demand for existing supply as well as for extended or new services.

Content of the study: In order to further promote entrepreneurship among women, it is crucial to have institutional support mechanisms that deliver the services needed by WE in a customer-oriented way. The study will examine the needs, perceptions and aspirations of the WE as well as analyse to **what extent the present supply of support services corresponds with the actual needs and demands of WE**. It encompasses an analysis of the demand-side as well as of the supply-side. On the one hand, the needs and the situation of the WE shall be examined, particularly concerning their growth pattern and perspectives. On the other hand, the existing provision of support initiatives shall be looked at. The study will accordingly strive to:
- identify **successful strategies** to promote WE that can be replicated and further developed (good practices)
- identify **challenges (gaps)** concerning the coverage of the existing support initiatives (in terms of outreach, content and impact)

---

[68] As an example, there are 9.1 million women-owned enterprises in the US, and in terms of employment creation and sales they are growing at twice the rate of male-owned enterprises.

In particular, the study will identify strategies that encourage the WE to upscale within the sub-sectors they are in as well as to consider expanding strategies into linked or new sectors.

Outcomes of the study: As a result of the above-described analysis, the following outputs shall be delivered by the study:

- an **overview** of the situation and perceptions of WE concerning their economic roles and their enterprises and the factors influencing them;
- an **overview** of the present supply of support initiatives for WE
- suggestions for immediate, **small-scale, one-time interventions** aimed at overcoming gaps as well as for pilot interventions which can help strengthen and upscale WE (3 to 4 interventions expected)
- a **summary of the lessons learned**, including recommendations for action at the policy-level (government policies, donor programs, NGOs, private sector) concerning the formulation and implementation of strategies to promote WE in Pakistan, as well as the documentation of 20 significant cases / profiles of women-owned enterprises

Methodology: The study aims to obtain the above results by referring to two major sources of information: first hand data collection, and the review of secondary data and documentation. First, to explore the demand-side (i.e. the **needs, aspirations and perceptions of the WE**) first hand data collection will be undertaken. A **field survey**, based on a sample of 150 WE, at various levels (micro, small and medium) will be undertaken. The working **definition** of a WE is as follows: A women-owned enterprise is an enterprise in which women are the majority owners and which operates from dedicated business premises other than their residential dwelling. This definition, by excluding the lower end of the scale of microenterprises, deliberately gears the attention of the survey on those enterprises, which have a certain potential for growth and upgrading. More than half of the sample (approx. 50-66 per cent) will belong to three sectors or sub-sectors (yet to be designated).

The findings of the survey will be underpinned and put in context by a thorough analysis of the available secondary data on WE in Pakistan.

Second, to obtain information on the nature of the existing support initiatives, a review of past and ongoing efforts to promote and support women's entrepreneurship through policies, programmes and the legal framework will be undertaken. It will be based on the available materials (including training manuals and evaluation reports), taking account of both women-specific and generic initiatives. Consideration should also be given to national efforts to implement the Beijing Platform of Action (1995), as well as Beijing Plus 5 documents and submissions to the UN-Convention on Elimination of all Forms of Discrimination Against Women (CEDAW).

Additionally, key informants of selected support initiatives will be consulted to obtain some first hand information on strategies and concepts. The limited scope of the research project does not allow for a second survey based on a sample of supporting institutions.

Structure of the survey:

The survey intends to provide answers in particular to the following questions:

- What do the women entrepreneurs need (e.g. in the form of support, assistance, etc.) to be able to implement their plans?
- What factors are working against implementing these plans and achieving these aspirations (negative force field analysis)?
- What forms of support and assistance do the women entrepreneurs need to overcome these barriers and obstacles?
- What costs can be attributed to getting around or overcoming these negative factors – e.g. "buying in" services; opportunity costs associated with lost sales; higher costs for materials, credit, transportation, etc
- How is growth perceived? – in general; specifically and/or in quantitative terms; and what is the stated/planned growth path?
- Are they content with their growth patterns and achievements?
- What do they see as the major obstacles to growth and expansion? What gender-related factors influence such constraints?

- How do they view the role of Government in facilitating and promoting their enterprises? What are the three (3) major roles they would to see Government playing?

Two **crosscutting focuses** are information on the status quo of the WE as well as information on the changes they consider being necessary in the future to improve their situation.

A. Questions concerning the **status quo** are: Who are the WE? What are their motives? What are their aspirations? How do they perceive themselves – as entrepreneurs or as family members (mothers, sisters, daughters) or both in equal terms? What is their enterprise like (performance past and expected / planned)? With whom are they communicating, cooperating?

B. Questions concerning **their perceptions on necessary changes, needs, gaps / deficiencies of the status quo** are: What do they think of the existing support structure? What do they need according to their perception? What kind of changes would they suggest or do they perceive to be most important / urgent?

The **survey** will investigate the following aspects, categorized in four thematic subgroups:

Profile of the entrepreneur as individual:
- The profile of the women entrepreneurs – age; level of education; marital status: number and age of children, prior work experience; place of origin;
- The attitudes and motivations of the women entrepreneurs – motives for starting the enterprises.
- The aspirations and plans of the women entrepreneurs
- What factors are working in favour of implementing these plans and achieving these aspirations (positive force field analysis) – including internal (e.g. personality, skills, etc.) and external (economic, cultural, family, etc.) factors?
- What is their level of awareness on business policy and regulatory matters? Do they consider laws, policies and regulations as major obstacles – how and why? What (if any) administrative obstacles, harassment or rent-seeking activities have they experienced from officials?

Profile of the entrepreneur as member of a household
- What relevance has the enterprise for the household in terms of income?
- On what does the WE invest / spend the profits from the enterprise?
- How do the other members of the household see the enterprise?
- What role does the husband/male family member play in supporting the business?
- What proportion of WE's time is spent in the business and in the home/household? How do they balance their household/family responsibilities and their business work? Is there conflict or complementarities?
- Who helps with the household and family work?
- Is anyone paid for child-minding or house-keeping (if so, how much)?
- How many hours does the husband (male partner) spend in household or family work?
- What are the occupations of the other household members (wage work, self-employed, reproductive work)?

Profile of the enterprise:
- The profile of the woman's enterprise - location of business; sector/subsector; date of establishment; enterprise assets: amount of investment: technology used: employment (women and men, full-time, part-time, paid and unpaid family workers); and other relevant descriptive information.
- Performance of the enterprises – trends and patterns in growth or decline - successes and failures; factors which have contributed to growth or decline; baseline of "today" – how was performance one year ago? (better/same/worse) employment? Profits? Customers? Expectations for one year in the future.
- The management and decision-making structure within the enterprise – work division between the entrepreneurs, her family members and paid employees; responsibility structure; who plans, makes management decisions, hiring new employees, purchasing, marketing and selling, public contact, investment decisions, business expansion ideas, etc.
- What management styles do the women entrepreneurs adopt? – hierarchical or vertical; participatory or autocratic; which do they find more effective and productive? (Some examples from other studies will be provided to guide the research team.)
- What are their marketing strategies, techniques and contacts? How do they form business linkages with suppliers/customers/competitors? Who controls these linkages and structures?
- What competition does the enterprise face? – from what other businesses? From what regions? How do they cope with this competition?

- The enterprise and professional needs (concentrate on non-financial) of the women entrepreneurs – e.g. General management; Skills development; Technology; Markets and marketing; International trade and exporting; Production; Procurement; Human resource management; ICTs;
- The financial requirements of the entrepreneur – Sources and amounts of credit: What are the immediate financial requirements? How have they been addressed? What gaps remain? What problems have there been? What lessons can be drawn?

Networks and contacts with other businesses or organisations / institutions:
- Affiliations – membership of professional and business associations, clubs and networks (including Chambers of Commerce and associations of women entrepreneurs); what services they provide; how representative they are; and some indications of their effectiveness; employers' organizations and Chambers of Commerce; Government/public sector service providers; INGOs and NGOs; women entrepreneur associations; specific (donor-assisted) programmes and projects; informally (specify); spouse, male relations, children and other family (specify); friends (specify).
- What is the communication and contact structure? Who carries out the negotiation functions? – negotiating with suppliers, agents, distributors, transport companies, customers, intermediaries, banks, Government agencies; dealing with issues relating to the employees (e.g. pay levels, disciplinary matters, etc.); who helps to obtain access to markets and market opportunities?

Use of existing offers / services:
- The existing sources of (non-financial) support and assistance availed of by the women entrepreneurs – including support from suppliers and customers ("business to business");

Duties and Responsibilities: Under the administrative supervision of the ILO Area Office (Islamabad) and technical guidance of the Senior Gender Specialist at ILO/SAAT New Delhi, and the Senior Specialist on Women's Entrepreneurship Development in the InFocus Programme, IFP/SEED, Geneva the consultant(s) will be required to carry out the impact study of women entrepreneurship programmes and prepare a draft report as described above. The draft report would need to be revised to incorporate the comments received from ILO.

The draft report should be written in English, around 50 pages long (with additional documentation on the survey and other materials and specific information provided in the annex to the report). The draft report should be submitted for review within two months of the signing of the contract, and necessary changes as suggested by the ILO should be made within 2 weeks of them being received by the consultant(s). The ILO will have exclusive rights to the report. (The ILO IFP/SEED will provide guidelines on the format to be adopted in preparing the report.)

Qualifications Desired: The consultant(s) should be knowledgeable in entrepreneurship development and women's development issues in general, and must have had previously prepared/published/presented in related technical areas, and these should be available for review by the ILO before the work is started. S/he should possess very good writing and speaking ability in English.

Appendix H - Summary Project Outline

Project Title: Creating an Information hub for Women Entrepreneurs (WEs) in Pakistan

Duration: 12 months

Starting Date: March 2003

Geographical Coverage: **Pakistan**
Project Language: English/Urdu

Executing Agency: International Labour Organization (ILO)

Implementing partners: To be agreed (from the list below)

Other Institutional Partners:

Small and Medium Enterprises Development Agency (SMEDA)
First Women Bank Limited (FWBL)
Ministry of Women Development (MoWD);
Ministry of Science and Technology (MoST);
Ministry of Planning and Development (P&D);
Export Promotion Bureau (EPB);
Agricultural Development Bank of Pakistan (ADBP);
Employers Federation of Pakistan (EFP);
SME Bank;
Board of Investment (BOI);
Punjab Small Industries Corporation (PSIC);
Sindh Small Industries Corporation (SSIC);
Sarhad Small Industries Development Board (SSIDB);
Directorate of Industries Balochistan (DIB);
Pakistan Poverty Alleviation Fund (PPAF);
Micro Finance (Khushhali) Bank;
National Rural Support Programme (NRSP);
Aga Khan Rural Support Programme (AKRSP);
Gender Equality Umbrella project (GEUP) of UNDP;
Gender Equity Project (GEP) of Department for International Development (DFID);
Association of Business, Professional and Agriculture Women;
Marketing Association of Pakistan (MAP);
Pakistan Association of Women Entrepreneurs (PAWE);
Women Entrepreneurs Cell of Lahore Chamber of Commerce and Industry (LCCI);
Federation of Pakistan Chambers of Commerce and Industry (FPCCI);
Women Studies Centre of University of the Punjab; University of Peshawar; University of Karachi; Quaid-e-Azam University; Islamabad; First Women's University;
Department of Women Development and Social Welfare, Government of Punjab.

Budget: US$ 30,000 (estimated)

Background and Justification

A recent study by ILO highlights 3 major areas of weakness in the development of women's businesses in Pakistan. The study is based upon a survey of 150 women entrepreneurs (WEs) and the survey report identifies (i) lack of business information; (ii) a low level of marketing knowledge and skills; and (iii) poor networking and representation as three major constraints.

(i) Lack of business information

The survey shows the lack of information as a major impediment for women in starting and growing a business. This is the result of government's poor capacity to consolidate scattered information, streamline it for the targeted clientele, and disseminate it effectively. The problem is further exacerbated by the limited outreach of various business development agencies (many of which are to be found in the public sector) in servicing their micro and small-scale enterprise (MSE) clients, especially women. The knowledge that women entrepreneurs have about the policy, legal and regulatory environment hence remains inadequate. The survey reveals that more than 60% of the businesswomen in the survey did not know about government policies related to investments, trade and export promotion, income and sales tax, concessionary finance and labour laws.

The lack of knowledge about certain government regulations is even more pronounced, as is manifested by the fact that 100% of the sample of women entrepreneurs did not know about the Statutory Regulatory Ordinances (SROs) that are issued by the Central Bureau of Revenue (CBR) for a variety of fiscal concessions available to support business and commercial activity. The information that women entrepreneurs have regarding government training and technical institutes is also inadequate as merely 30% about Pakistan Council for Scientific and Industrial Research; 25% about Punjab Vocational Training Council (PVTC); 21% knew about Technical Education and Vocational Training Authority (TEVTA); 9% about Scientific and Technological Development Corporation, and 5% each about National Productivity Organization (NPO) and Scientific and Technological Development Corporation (STEDEC). With regard to more global trade issues, of the women entrepreneurs sampled, 53% had no idea about the World Trade Organization (WTO) and they were unable to proffer an opinion on how Pakistan's accession to the WTO is going to affect their business.

(ii) Marketing knowledge and skills

The marketing modes and coverage of women in business also indicate information gaps of different types. The survey results show that as many as 79% of the WEs are selling their products and services exclusively in the local markets. They appear to be unaware of product-market divide and they are remote from lucrative domestic and international markets, not only geographically, but also in terms of their knowledge and awareness of what and where these markets are and their actual ability to access and competitively sell in those markets. Their over-reliance on informal marketing channels comes out as another weakness of marketing. Only 10% said that they make use of intermediaries for marketing their products and services. Various informal and formal channels were reported as the dominant modes of marketing, such as personal contacts (38%), telephone campaigns (26%) and exhibitions (24%). Their over-dependence on informal channels not only limits their access to formal markets, but also undermines their bargaining power in business transactions in the absence of formal and enforceable business and legal contracts.

(iii) Poor networking and representation

Another feature of women's businesses in Pakistan is their isolated working situation in which they do not interact extensively with the relevant business associations, chambers of commerce, networking groups, or other related organizations. Only 13% of the WEs in the surveyed sample belonged to some related networking groups, while 69% revealed that had never been in touch with

sample did not know about these organizations; 17% were of the opinion that their services are not so good; 7% thought that the range of services provided by such organizations is bad, while only 8% said that they are good. Only 3%WEs had received any kind of business help from these networking organizations, while the remaining 97% had not received any help from them in the past 3 years.

The problem of the women entrepreneurs' relative isolation becomes even worse when in the socio–cultural milieu of Pakistan, where the mobility of women is not very well accepted, thus hampering their movements for business purposes. Coupled with these problems, is the prevalent problem that is related with the mechanics of working and interacting with government departments. The bureaucratic and time-consuming procedures severely retard WEs' ease of access to the business development services provided by different government institutions. This also arises from the significant mismatch between the supply business services and the demand from micro and small-scale entrepreneurs, particularly women. The demand for business services by the entrepreneurs – and women entrepreneurs in particular - is generally multifaceted, as business is a complex game. But each government agency tends to specialize in one specific service - e.g. EPB in export marketing; SME Bank in financial services; SMEDA in non-financial business services; BOI in investments, and so on. The absence of a one-stop-shop mechanism makes it difficult for entrepreneurs in general, and WEs in particular given the added obstacles that they face, to run from one agency to the other to get information and help.

Having highlighted the gaps in the supply of services, the report also indicates a number of demand-side issues raised by the WEs in the sample. Support with marketing, finance and networking come out as major demands of the WEs. Furthermore, almost half of businesswomen indicated that they intend to expand the use of Information and Communication Technologies (ICTs) in their business. It is interesting to note that the average of computer literates among the businesswomen in the sample is much higher (68%) as compared to the national computer literacy average (16%) for women. This issue is worthy of further investigation, but provides a rough estimate of better computer literacy of WEs.

This summary highlights the information and knowledge gaps, as well as the lack of networking, as the main hindrances in the development of women's businesses in Pakistan. The relatively narrow focus of government institutions (BDS, skills training, finance, etc.) and the restricted mobility of women also calls for a solution that is culturally consistent with the Pakistani situation. A one-stop-shop solution, in the form of an information hub hosted at the World Wide Web (http://www) comes out as a logical solution for all these issues. This will not only serve the purpose of WEs getting general business information, improved market access and enhanced networking, but will also facilitate the various government and private sector institutions to expand their outreach to assist and support both women and men in accordance with the substance and spirit of their respective mandates. An information hub for WEs is thus proposed to address these gaps, in particular overcoming the "product-market divide" that affects many small-scale women entrepreneurs. The information hub should include following necessary information:

1. Consolidated information, addresses and contact persons of government agencies engaged in the provision of financial and non-financial business development services, with links to web pages where available. Also links to chambers of commerce and industry; related private sector institutions; business associations; women focused business networking groups; associations of women entrepreneurs; national and international networking forums.

2. On-line information on various aspects of the policy, regulatory and legal environment as pertinent to doing business in Pakistan, and as largely being provided through SMEDA.

3. Feasibility studies for starting micro, small and medium businesses, with a particular focus on women – thereby tapping in to accumulated expertise development by FWBL among others.

4. Information on the various stages of the enterprise life cycle and related issues, with particular reference to gender-based issues as they relate to women in business.

5. International business and export opportunities, and information on the knowledge and systems that need to be in place for WEs to enter and stay in the markets

6. Global value chain analysis as it relates to enhancing the opportunities for the women focused businesses to enter competitive and lucrative domestic and international market, thereby building upon the work of the EPB.

7. Latest information and updates on global changes in the international markets.

8. Networking opportunities with similar business in Pakistan and other countries, e.g. for arrangements such as sub-contracting, joint marketing, etc.

9. Information on training and development opportunities as they relate particularly to women entrepreneurs in Pakistan.

10. Linking in with matchmaking services and sub-contracting exchanges.

11. A section on Frequently Asked Questions (FAQs) that have direct relevance to the specified target groups.

12. Networking with the international organizations such as the ILO among others, that work for the promotion of business development by both women and men.

The development of the web-site will be complemented by web-site awareness seminars and short training programs targeting women to help them in identifying and assessing market opportunities; improving access to markets; practical marketing skills on distribution channels and strategies; export marketing; policy and regulatory issues, etc.

Objectives

Overall objective: To contribute to employment creation, sustainable livelihoods, poverty reduction, and improvements in the bargaining power of women entrepreneurs in Pakistan.

Immediate objectives:

a) To help women entrepreneurs overcome the information gaps relating to the business and economic scenario in Pakistan, with respect to the socio-cultural traditions of Pakistan;

b) To improving the women entrepreneurs' access to lucrative domestic and international markets access, and develop their capacity for entering into new markets and remaining competitive in a digital world;

c) To enhance prospects for representation and networking by and among women entrepreneurs in Pakistan, taking account of various obstacles to mobility, etc.

d) To build upon and provide a tangible manifestation of the signed MOU between SMEDA and FWBL (March 2002), and mainstream issues relating to economic empowerment of women and gender equality into the programmes and activities of both organizations.

Expected outputs:

i. An information intermediary for business development services for WEs, especially in the fields of marketing and networking;

ii. Reduced communication costs for WEs;

iii. Increased access to technology use by WEs;

iv. Increased availability of information by WEs;

v. Reduced transaction costs for WEs;

vi. Lowered barriers to entry for WEs in the global markets;

vii. Information exchanges by different organizations involved in promoting and supporting women entrepreneurship in Pakistan;

viii. Linkages with the international women organizations and other international bodies.

Indicators of Achievement

- Online registration of 300 women entrepreneurs by December 2003

- Improvement of 4 selected groups of sector-specific business activity (each group comprising of 3 or more WEs and one group from each province) by training and handholding to secure sustainable access to domestic and international markets;

- A range of the following materials developed, with Urdu translation and uploading to the web:

  - Women specific materials relating to policy, regulatory and legal issues;

  - Feasibility studies for starting a business;

  - Issues relating to the Enterprise Life Cycle;

  - Training materials on entrepreneurship, with particular reference to women's entrepreneurship development and gender equality issues;

  - Synopsis of government institutions, contact persons and their links;

  - Materials on identifying and assessing market opportunities, improving access to markets, marketing channels and strategies and export marketing.

- 50 WEs establish links with the national and international networking organizations;

- Improvement in 100 women businesses with contributions through inputs from the website.

- Assimilation of lessons emerging from this pilot project will be sought among project implementing partners, as well as among other agencies cooperating with the project.

- As this is a pilot project activity, clear indications of donor assistance (including newly funded projects related to this pilot) will be sought as indicators.

Proposed Implementation Strategy

The programme will be implemented through an institutional arrangement between the International Labour Organization (ILO) and designated partner organizations (as selected from the list on the cover page). The implementational arrangements would aim to build upon the existing Memorandum of Understanding (MOU) signed between SMEDA and FWBL (8 March 2002, International Women's Day). This will become the first tangible manifestation under that umbrella cooperation. A joint workshop will be held in the early months of project implementation to agreed and establish the modalities of cooperation between the three partners.

Target Groups

The intended direct beneficiaries are women entrepreneurs in micro, small and medium-scale enterprises operating as producers, exporters, traders and service providers in Pakistan. The project will address the significant information gaps (as detailed above) by raising the WEs' awareness about policy, regulatory and legal aspects of doing business. It will also help them in identifying and assessing market opportunities, improving access to markets and networking with business and other related organizations. It will contribute to them improving their product development, production operations and logistical support, as well as enhance international networking. The project will indirectly help the other (large number of) partner organizations from the government and private sector to be able to attract and service more clients (particularly WEs), network with similar organizations, and build their capacity to carry out their functions in a better way so as to meet the demands and needs of both women and men in business.

Institutional framework

The ILO would hope to involve key players in this field, such as the Women Entrepreneurs' Cell that has been created in the Policy, Planning and Strategy Department of SMEDA, and FWBL and other partner organizations. Institutional arrangements would provide for arranging meetings, planning schedules and identifying more partner organizations to participate in and contribute to project implementation. This could include, inter alia, the Marketing Association of Pakistan (MAP), Ministry of Women Development and Social Welfare, and the various departments of provincial governments that could facilitate the execution of the project.

Planning, Monitoring, Evaluation and Impact Assessment

The project has been proposed and planned as an outcome of the ILO-sponsored study and a subsequent workshop of stakeholders held in Lahore, in February 2002. The ILO study systematically surveyed the situation and circumstances of 150 women entrepreneurs, and indicated gaps requiring attention. At the Lahore workshop, participants emphasized the necessity of such web site and recommended to make it an information hub for the economic empowerment of women in general, and women's entrepreneurship development in particular. Hence the idea was conceived on the basis of original research and the consultative and participatory planning process at the Lahore workshop. The next planning phase will be a joint meeting of the stakeholders to decide the modalities of cooperation for this pilot project activity.

A baseline situation will be compiled at the beginning of the project, and this will be used to monitor and measure progress and impact over time. Regular monitoring of the project will be carried out by ILO office in Pakistan in association with ILO-SAAT based in New Delhi and IFP/SEED based in Geneva.

ILO's institutional and implementational partners will be expected to generate quarterly progress reports for the review of ILO. A mid-term review of the project will be carried out by ILO headquarters six months into project implementation, and a final (terminal) report will be prepared after 12 months of operation.

Appendix I

WORKSHOP RECOMMENDATIONS
Launching Ceremony of draft report on
"Women Entrepreneurs in Pakistan"
A Study to understand and improve their Bargaining Power"
15 February, 2002, Avari Hotel, Lahore

- A comprehensive development package for the Women Entrepreneurs (WEs) should be formulated that includes basic information on business concepts, as well as the development of related expertise for doing business and providing information on the government and non-government resources that are available.

- The media in Pakistan has a very important role to play in bridging the information gaps that exist between the would-be women entrepreneurs and the existing business and market opportunities. Both print and electronic media should be effectively used to disseminate this information.

- At present, the outreach of various Government institutions is very poor and many people do not know the kind of services that they are offering. The same is true for the various women business forums and associations, as well as special cells/units (if any) that have been established at the chambers of commerce and industry.

- Information needs to be collected and collated regarding the women entrepreneurs in Pakistan. The Export Promotion Bureau (EPB) has a directory of women entrepreneurs, but few people know of it. Similarly, First Women's Bank Limited (FWBL) is trying to get some database of women entrepreneurs. The United States (US) Consulate has sponsored the development of a women entrepreneurship module and this information was shared at this workshop. More meetings/forums and information exchanges, such as this one, are needed, where the stakeholders can sit together and share information. In this way, the wheel does not have to be reinvented every time women's entrepreneurship development is being discussed.

- There is a need to have a Women Entrepreneurship Institute in Pakistan so that it can become the focal point of all the WED activity.

- The information regarding starting and sustaining a business is scattered and is generally only limited to big cities. New ways need to be devised to improve the access to this information.

- The role of networking organizations needs to be strengthened.

- Finance has come up time and again as a major constraint and it is necessary to look deeper into this issue and see what are the hurdles in terms of regulations (prudential regulations), procedures (snags) and requirements (collateral etc.).

- We need to have a deeper cut into the existing regulatory environment and see if there are any hidden or obvious biases that affect women entrepreneurship.

- This study should be taken as a pilot project. Similar studies should be done in the other three provinces to have a national flavor and to see what are the common denominators as far as the gaps and opportunities are concerned. On the other hand a similar study should be carried out for men entrepreneurs with the same set of questions to exactly benchmark it.

- There should be Awareness raising campaigns through print & electronic media, e.g. case studies and media projection be made of other countries where women entrepreneurs have thrived. A good example could be that of Indonesia where the socio-economic conditions and religion has been the same as that of Pakistan.

- WEs awareness raising should be done through the recently elected women councilors of the district assemblies. Women councilors should be sensitized and given information on the opportunities and they should be the change agents along with NGOs and other social agents.

- Business Forums for women entrepreneurs need to be strengthened.

- There should be some forum where the men and women business forums could interact and they do not start working in isolation.

- First Women Bank should adopt an aggressive approach of outreach and handhold women entrepreneurs.

- Pakistan economy has been in a down turn since 1990s and a series of exogenous and endogenous shocks have resulted in shrinkage of GDP and rising poverty. The evidence from survey also shows that the rate of We has accelerated. This is about time to hit on the conservative mindset and start propagating that women entrepreneurship is needed on the basis of sheer economic necessity.

- We need to develop strong linkages and collaboration amongst the academic institutions, development practitioners and various government and international agencies.

- We must prepare and offer short and extended developmental programs for women entrepreneurs at different institutions and locations and especially with the Home Economics Colleges, M.BA classes and women Studies Centers of the universities.

- conduct extensive and intensive research on women entrepreneurship in Pakistan

- Develop stakeholders networks to bring them out of isolation.

- Arrange exclusive exhibitions at small places where women can sell their products/ services; Special Sunday markets could be one option.

- The women should be encouraged to take part in the non-conventional businesses and they should be urged to specialize in their trades.

- Develop a new breed of role models.

- Single platform (website /portal) for women that would project, educate and inform women entrepreneurs in Pakistan. It would disseminate information on various incentive/schemes launched by the public sector, features would include; virtual exhibitions, IT training, forum, helpdesk, presence of donor and credit agencies in Pakistan, etc. This will serve as 24 hours access/marketing connect and will be a low cost marketing tool.

www.ingramcontent.com/pod-product-compliance
Lightning Source LLC
Chambersburg PA
CBHW081157270326

41930CB00014B/3192